KNOWING BETTER

How knowing God will change everything. **EVERYTHING.**

JENNIFER WINQUIST

BEING BETTER, INC.
SIOUX CITY, IA . WWW.BEINGBETTER.ORG

Published by Being Better Media.

ISBN: 978-0-578-81710-1

To order additional copies of this publication, contact us at Being Better, Inc. P.O. Box 5105, Sioux City, IA 51104. Phone: 712-301-4341.
Email: Contact@BeingBetter.org. Order online at www.BeingBetter.org

Printed in the United States of America.

Cover photo background with backpack boy by Vladislav Babienko on Unsplash along with mom and daughter by Sai DeSilva, woman wearing hat by Brooke Cagle, elderly man by David Sinclair, woman with floral shirt by Mark Timberlake, man in suit by Benjamin Rascoe, and man crouching by Luigi Estuye. Military man by Pixel-Shot and prisoner by LightField Studios /Shutterstock.com.

CONTENTS

What's coming up

ABOUT THE AUTHOR

KNOWING HIM

will change your life. I know because He changed mine.

The author
Jennifer Winquist

As someone who grew up in a Christian home going to church EVERY Sunday, you'd think I'd have this faith thing all figured out by the time I was in my 40s. I would have told you I did. Right up until my life was train-wrecked. Then I realized my faith was all an illusion. Even to me.

I was really good at faking it. Pretending like I understood what I was SURE everybody else at church knew — what the Bible said and how to live the way Jesus did. Suddenly, I HAD to know for myself.

I went on a journey with God and I met Jesus really for the first time. I found there was so much that I either didn't know or that I was getting wrong. I spent time with Jesus everyday and read the Bible like my life depended on it. It did.

Today my entire life is changed. Where I was before was a terrifying place where I thought nothing would EVER be different. Couldn't be fixed. But God. He came and got me from despair and brought me to a place of confidence and love. I went from being scared and worried to having complete peace and living a joy-filled life every single day. I learned how to trust God with absolutely everything. EVERYTHING.

On this incredible journey with Him over the last 10 years, I see how few people REALLY know Him. Honestly, most people who consider themselves Christians are just like I was — saying they follow Jesus without having any idea how to really do that. They want to be different, feel fulfilled, be whole, but they don't know how to let God be in control so things might actually get better. Others are afraid to admit they truly don't know what God wants or they're scared He'll want more than they want to give. We are afraid of what our lives will look like. Who we'll be.

Let me put your fears to rest. When we seek God with everything we have and learn how to authentically follow Jesus we will get a life that is more than we can fathom. Jeremiah 29:13 says, *You will seek me and find me, when you seek me with all your heart.* The secret is, when you find God you will find yourself too. The you that God had planned all along for you to be. The you that is hopeful and happy. You will like that person VERY much.

This study will help you learn exactly HOW to have a life-changing relationship with God. It will be a hard journey at times, but it will be worth absolutely everything! Come and meet Jesus. Come and get to know God. Knowing Him will change your life — it will change EVERYTHING!

May God bless you like crazy!

Jennifer

HEY!

What you'll need to know going in

I am so excited that you are even considering doing this study! I wanted to give you a heads up as to what you'll need to know in order to get the most out of this and some instructions so your experience is a good one.

Who this is for. You — if you are someone who wants or needs their life to be different. Someone who doesn't know a thing about Jesus, church, or anything religious or someone who's been a member for decades. Someone who is willing to listen, learn, and ultimately change. Someone who thinks it might be a good thing to let Jesus show you how to do life. Someone who wants to get to know God and to hang out with Jesus.

Be all in. If you truly want to get everything out of this you can, then don't take any short cuts. Do all the exercises as they come up. Don't think you'll come back and do them later — it won't be the same experience as doing it in the moment. Look up all the verses. Sit with Jesus and talk. Spend time.

Don't rush. Do one day at a time so you can absorb it all — roll it around. Process it.

Write it down. As much as you can, write your answers (responses to Jesus) down. Something extra happens in the writing.

Supplies. You'll need a Bible. The lessons primarily use *The Holy Bible New International Version* (2011). If you have another version that's okay, but areas you fill in the blanks may be worded a little differently. (See pg. 150 if you need help choosing a Bible and how to access a free online Bible.) Other than that, just grab something to write with.

Journal/take notes. There are pages in the back of the workbook to jot down thoughts and make notes as you'd like. Journaling is a great way to process what you're experiencing. Just write out what you're thinking and feeling — what you want to tell yourself or say to Jesus.

I hope God blesses you like crazy as you turn each page! I've been praying for each step you'll take!

WEEK 1

TIME FOR A CHANGE

This could potentially be the most important week of your life. Seriously. If you are here, something has been stirring in you. You want or need something to change. (If you don't sense that and are doing this because your small group is, or someone else thinks you should, think about what YOU want. Be mindful that in order to grow we need to allow ourselves to be vulnerable, to get uncomfortable. If you're not up for growth and change this may not be the study for you.) If you're already realizing you're not where you want to be in life then you are absolutely in the right place.

For this first week, we've got some ground work to cover. No matter where you are in life, no one is at a disadvantage because we are starting at the beginning. If you think you've "been there, done that" you may be surprised at what you missed (depending on how you grew up and what you were taught...and what might have been left out or watered down). This week will be a little different from upcoming weeks as some of it will be more instructional than study work.

For those of you who are here because you have a big problem, an ongoing struggle, or are praying some hope lies in here for you, take heart. This is exactly what you need. God promises us that we don't have to worry (about anything), we don't have to be afraid (of anything), that we can have confidence in our lives and future, and that we can trust Him to take care of everything. Things can change — everything can change.

Day 1

WHY YOU'RE HERE

A GOOD POINT

Real love doesn't meet you at your best. It meets you in your mess.
-Unknown

If you're experiencing a hard time right now, it's easy to think that no one understands what you're going through. That is a tiny bit true, but mostly it's not. While we all have a situation that is unique to us because *we* are unique — we think different, feel different, and have different backgrounds and experiences — there is always someone who has been through what you're dealing with. It is a strange thing that knowing we aren't suffering alone gives us comfort. But it's that idea we came to know well during the pandemic — that we were all in it together — that gives us strength. Know that you aren't alone.

The Bible says, *"No temptation has overtaken you except what is common to mankind. And God is faithful; he will not let you be tempted beyond what you can bear. But when you are tempted, he will also provide a way out so that you can endure it."* (1 Corinthians 10:13) While this scripture is talking about getting caught up in sin, the same holds true for those who are experiencing any struggle.

I know one of you right now is thinking, *"You don't understand, my situation is different."* OR, *"You think you know what I'm dealing with, but you don't!"* If you think you are some special sort of screwed up, you're not. God has it covered. Just to be clear, God knows it all. God knows what your PTSD is doing to your life — to your mind. He knows how devastating your divorce is. He understands your overwhelming grief. He gets that you feel hopeless in your depression. He sees that your addiction is sucking the life out of you. He knows what you did to that person. To that child. To yourself. What others did to you. He saw everything you'd never want to be made public. He knows your shame, your guilt, your worry, and your fear. He knows what you need and what you deserve.

If you think you're some special sort of screwed up, you're not.

The amazing part is, He is able to fix it all. To forgive it all. To comfort you, to build you back up, to kick down the walls, love you, fill you with joy and peace and restore you. To give you purpose and hope. To give you eternity. Yes, yes, yes, I said YOU! God is looking right at you with this message of hope. In the coming days and weeks, we will unpack HOW all this happens and what you have to do to bask in the reality of it.

Are you ready? Today, we are starting where you are. Who you are in this moment. We'll want to come back here when it's all said and done and see how things have changed so let's put this info into our time capsule. The most important thing right now is to be totally honest with yourself. Nobody else needs to see this. This is just between you and God (and He already knows it all anyhow so let it out).

You are here for a reason, maybe for a few reasons. Read through the descriptions below and check the one (or ones) that ring true, circle any specific struggles, and write in anything that isn't listed that comes to mind.

Today, ____________, I am:
date

- ☐ Desperate/On the brink of hopelessness
  Something has to change! I'm in big trouble!

- ☐ Circling the pit
  I'm out of the pit and trying to stay out. I'm afraid of what will happen if...

- ☐ Wanting more/Realizing something's missing
  I feel unfulfilled. I worry. I'm afraid a lot. I don't have much/any peace.

- ☐ Losing faith
  God seems to show up for other people but not me. I don't understand why...

- ☐ Other ____________________

While it may feel a little discouraging to own those feelings, know that those negatives can be a thing of the past if you do the work and stick it out. I don't say that flippantly, but knowingly. My "freedom" came in fits and starts, not all at once like I would have liked. My road was not a smooth one or a straight one. I very often found myself circling back on dark roads that I should have never gone down — didn't need to go down — but because I had a partner on the journey (that would be Jesus), I always got back to the path with the light shining on it. I fell into the pit more times than I'd like to admit. Way more. But, God would pull me up at just the right time and give me hope — and that gave me strength for the next time I fell, the next time I doubted. He fed me truth and I learned I could trust Him...with everything... every time. In time, Jesus and I filled the pit in and tapped it down with a steam roller. No more pit.

Who I am *now* is not even close to who I *was*. The new me is the one God had planned all along. The one who isn't afraid, isn't worried, isn't lost. The one who feels whole. Healed.

In the coming days, you'll decide if you want to take your own journey with God. Let me put it all out there for you: If you are in a hard place, your journey may be longer than you want it to be. What I found out is that it will be exactly as long as you need it to be and every step of the way gets you closer to the goal and enjoying all the promises. Just know that long, hard journeys with God are worth everything and you will NEVER regret taking them. Your time with God will be unique and perfect...filled with adventure both amazing and difficult.

If that sounds a little unsettling, please, please, please hear me on this: If you want complete and total life change where EVERYTHING is how you want it to be (filled with unfailing love, peace, and joy — FOREVER), going all-in with God is the only way to get it. If you want an out-of-the-ordinary life, you have to take an out-of-the-ordinary road. If you are in a difficult place, you already know how to do hard. You can and will make it!

Here's another question for you.

What defines you?
Jot down some things that you find your identity in — what you view as positive things that describe who you are. List as many as you can. *(Examples: son, soldier, parent, farmer, political affiliation, social stance, etc.)*

Now, list some current struggles that you don't want to be part of your identity. *(Examples: addiction, disturbing thoughts, depression, lust, lack of purpose, anger, low self-esteem, poor, unloved, physical appearance, etc.)*

I've got one last question.

Which religious classification would you say you are right now?

- ☐ Christian
  I've personally invited Jesus to be in charge of my life.

- ☐ Non-Christian
  I have not personally told Jesus that I want Him to run my life.

Many things are important to us in life. We want people to think certain things about us — we don't always even care if they are true. Someone once said, *"People would rather look good than actually be good."* If people *think* we are kind or trustworthy we figure that's a win. Forget that we belittle our spouse or lied on our taxes. Yet, accepting false praise doesn't make us feel right — not deep down where it counts, where it eats at us. If we are ever going to be okay with who we are – authentically real, we'll have to put in the work. What I know from personal experience is that until something is a real problem, staring us down, we take the easy way. We let it go, put it off.

If you are engaged in a battle right now, I'm excited for you. People in a battle fight! They see what is at stake and they are motivated (aka: desperate) to win. Know that your battle plan is outlined in this book...and complete in God's book and we are going to show you how to find it, follow it, and conquer with it!

If you stick with it, you'll find that who you are all comes down to your relationship with one guy named Jesus. All of the other stuff you marked down about who you are (good and bad) may change a lot if you decide to go where He is going. Here's a hint: It's exactly where you want to go.

Some friends of ours told us about their brother. While only in his 50s, he was on Hospice care because of cancer complications. He didn't want anyone to visit him, just to watch him die. He wouldn't let anyone bring up the topic of salvation (getting to heaven) either. He was sure what he'd done in his life was unforgivable. He'd decided it was a settled matter. He died alone and bitter based on a complete lie.

Here is a trustworthy saying that deserves full acceptance: Christ Jesus came into the world to save sinners—of whom I am the worst. But God had mercy on me so that Christ Jesus could use me as a prime example of his great patience with even the worst sinners. Then others will realize that they, too, can believe in him and receive eternal life.
-Paul
1 Timothy 1:15-16

It's not about what you've done, it's about your desire to be forgiven for it. God's whole deal is fixing us broken people. In the Bible, Paul knew better than anyone what God would forgive. Before he met Jesus he fiercely went after Christians and was even a party to murdering them. Once he'd met Jesus he said, as far as sinners went, *"Christ Jesus came into the world to save sinners—of whom I am the worst."* (See the verse in the margin.) Yet, God made a way for our slate to be erased (we'll tell you how tomorrow...unless you can't wait). Here are a few things God says to assure us.

Hebrews 4:16: *Let us then approach God's throne of grace with confidence, so that we may receive mercy and find grace to help us in our time of need.*

Isaiah 32:17: *The fruit of that righteousness will be peace; its effect will be quietness and confidence forever.*

Psalm 16:11: *You make known to me the path of life; you will fill me with joy in your presence, with eternal pleasures at your right hand.*

Whether you're dealing with sin or other hard things in life, if you want your life to be changed, you just have to show up with God everyday. He loves you. He wants you to be all He made you to be. He has a great plan for you. You don't have to feel "less than" in any way. He is a God of completeness. Be all in with God and nothing will ever be the same.

Day 2

KNOWING I'M SAVED

A GOOD POINT

Salvation is free but it's the most valuable thing in the world.
-Unknown

As we discussed yesterday, we are starting at the beginning. It's interesting to note that most people view this beginning as what will happen in the end. Where we'll end up when this life is over. This is our beginning because it's from here on out.

Salvation. Being saved. Am I saved? Born again. How to go to heaven. These are some of the most important phrases of all time and if you're on the quest for answers and understanding or a deepening of faith, it's pretty imperative each of us knows where we stand on these. If you're here right now, it's likely not by accident. God has something to tell you and apparently you are ready to hear it.

All of those terms come down to one reality – how we'll spend eternity. When we think about the word "eternity" we think it's referring to our future – after we die – but, in God's plan, eternity starts now. By default, our destiny is death and hell because we are separated from God because we are sinners. Until we rectify that, our eternity won't change. **But God.** He made a way for us to become new and change our eternity – from here on out. **Are you ready to find out how?**

Depending what happens in this stepping off point, you'll want to make sure you've got enough uninterrupted time – 30 to 60 minutes. Give yourself time to focus on this – it is your eternity we're talking about after all.

TWO QUICK NOTES:

1. For those of you who aren't sure what to expect, maybe don't feel like you're good enough, are unsure how to change some bad thoughts and behaviors, and the past is weighing heavy – you are absolutely in the right place. Sometimes we know what we should want, but our "want to" seems to be broken. If all you've got is the desire to *want to* want the right things, that's enough. God can work with that.

2. For those who would say they are already saved, have accepted Jesus, are a Christian, or feel confident about heaven, you are also in the right place. As you'll read on the upcoming page, there may be a very good reason you're

here too. What's a half-hour out of your eternity to see if God wants you to hear something today?

Look at A and B below and read the option that best describes your situation. Step into your eternity!

A. I want to know how to get to heaven/I'm not saved:

Whether you have no clue who Jesus is, have never met God, or just have had a lack-luster journey so far you are in the right place. You are also in the right place if you think that you are so messed up, have done so much wrong that God couldn't possibly want you or let you into heaven. You are in the right place if you have prayed and nothing seems to happen and you think God doesn't care.

You are not here by accident. God loves you. That is a for sure thing. He has a plan for you that involves being forgiven of everything, starting fresh, living a whole and fulfilled life, and being with Him forever.

In the coming moments, you'll learn about God's plan and decide if you want to accept that plan for your life. Everyone has the option to accept or not. Jesus says the only criteria is that you are a sinner. Good thing we all qualify.

One thing I ask: Don't make a decision or jump out before the end. Make sure you get all the info so you know exactly what you want to do.

If this covers you, continue to the next page: Journeys always start...>>>

B. I already accepted Jesus/I feel pretty confident I'm going to heaven.

I pray that what you believe about your relationship with Jesus is right. As someone who went to church her whole life and thought her faith was rock solid, when a very difficult season came I realized I didn't know what I believed. I realized I really didn't know God personally. Sure, I prayed, but it wasn't change-your-life stuff. I realized that much of what I'd learned growing up wasn't right. That much of it had been dumbed down or sugar-coated. I realized I'd been robbed of so much. I don't want that for you.

If you don't currently have a close and deep, jaw-dropping walk with God, then I hope you'll humor me and go through this Salvation "How To" to make sure you're where you should be.

Remember, in Matthew 7:21 Jesus warns about the coming judgment, *"Not everyone who says to me, 'Lord, Lord,' will enter the kingdom of heaven, but only the one who does the will of my Father who is in heaven. Many will say to me on that day, 'Lord, Lord, did we not prophesy in your name and in your name drive out demons and in your name perform many miracles?' Then I will tell them plainly, 'I never knew you. Away from me, you evildoers!'"*

The people Jesus is talking about are people who thought they were good with God. They were wrong. Make sure you're not.

Journeys always start at the beginning

After interviewing many, many people over the years, do you want to know what we have in common when it comes to our faith - any faith? **We pretty much believe what we are told.** We'll continue to believe that until what we we're told doesn't pan out...doesn't hold water.

If you are here right now, it's likely you've noticed that something isn't quite right in your life, it feels like something is missing, or a dam just broke and you need to shore it up or you're going under. Perhaps you see that the way you've been going is a dead end. Whatever the reason, the only place to start a journey is at the beginning.

This isn't a figurative journey - it is as real as it gets. Make sure you are really here. What I mean is that I am not telling you a tale about a fictional journey, I'm helping you on yours. This journey will take you where you want to go. It's not where you *think* you want to go - it's where God has planned for you to go. **It is where everything falls into place, where you find answers, where you find yourself, and your purpose.**

Like every voyage, there needs to be a Captain, someone to take us on the adventure, the one who has charted the course. I'm not the Captain — Jesus is. I've just sailed with Him for a long time and I can help you for part of the journey. If you decide to take it.

The journey starts when you decide to let Him in.

Here's where we begin

Look at the room you are in. This is where you start. Now, look at the door. If you can't see it from where you are, just see it in your mind. Maybe you've seen that famous painting of Jesus standing outside of a door, knocking. There's a bit of a window in the door so you can see it's Him...not someone waiting to roll you in the bushes when you open it. If you study the image, you'll notice that there is no doorknob on Jesus' side. It's your job to open the door - not His.

By Warner Sallman (1892-1968)

The journey starts when you decide to let Him in.

If you are a normal human, you want to know who you're letting in — what the stipulations are of inviting Him in. You may have heard some people say that His offer is free. That is true. It doesn't mean it's easy and that it won't cost you *something*. So, let's find out if you want to open the door.

Get comfortable

If you haven't figured it out, this is a big decision. The biggest. If there are distractions around you this would be a good time to excuse yourself to a quiet place, turn off the TV, pull out the ear buds. This isn't something to do as a group. This is just between you and Him.

Right now, you are on the opposite side of the door from Jesus. Now, let me tell you some things about Him so you can determine if you want what He's offering you.

Jesus and I have been talking about you (otherwise known as praying). I wanted to make sure I told you about Him in just the right way. **In a nutshell, He is Everything. He is God's rescue plan. He is the How-To Manual.** He is *"the Way, the Truth, and the Life."* – John 14:6

What does that mean? He is the Way to go, the Example to follow, the Gateway into heaven. He is the Truth about your life, the Honesty you won't want to hear sometimes, and the Voice that comforts you and encourages you. He is the Life-giver, the Restorer of things once dead, and He is love, peace, and joy which makes life worth living.

So, what's He doing here knocking on your door? **He's coming to get you. To get you back.** Back from where? **Back from death.**

First, a little background

When God created man there was nothing wrong with us. God hung out with us, told us what to do, and things were good. Perfect in fact. Then, Adam and Eve sinned – did something God specifically told them not to do. It ruined everything. It ushered in death.

Because we were born from sinful people, we have sin just like them. It's an inherited trait. That trait separates us from God. Romans 3:23 says, *"All have sinned and fall short of the glory of God."*

All.

So, everyone of us has failed to make the grade. Want to know what the penalty is for that?

Romans 6:23 says, *"The wages of sin is death."* We think being dead is ceasing to be alive on planet Earth. That's not really it. True death is separation from God. Unless you have been restored by God, you are currently separated from Him – dead. Sooner or later, our bodies will physically die, yet our spirit will live on – we just change addresses from P.O. Box Earth to Heaven or Hell. If our sins haven't been paid for we go to Hell – that is true/ultimate death (being without God = ultimate despair/no hope). Yep, that sounds horrifying so let's move on. Thankfully, God has another option – one that can start today.

God knew we could not fix our sin problem, our being-dead problem, on our own. The Old Testament prophets (people who spoke for God) told that He would send a Savior – or Messiah…Christ. The New Testament tells that Jesus IS that Savior. Colossians 1:15 says, *"Christ is the visible image of the invisible God."* (NLT) Basically, God got into a human body to come and save us. Why?

Romans 5:8 says, *"God demonstrates His own love toward us, in that while we were yet sinners, Christ died for us."* Here's where a lot of people get it wrong. They think they have to clean up their act, stop doing this bad thing or that, before they come to God. If we could have fixed ourselves, we would have! God sent His son Jesus SO THAT we could get our act cleaned up.

When the Navy Seal crashes through the compound where you're being held prisoner you just go with him regardless of the state you are in. Okay? Your injuries and issues will be taken care of once you're en route.

In the Bible, Jesus says in John 3:16, *"For God so loved the world that He gave His one and only Son, that whoever believes in Him shall not perish but have eternal life."* God loves you. Do not miss that. He loves YOU and He wants YOU to live forever with Him. Jesus said it's not going to be just an ordinary life but, *"I have come that they may have life, and that they may have it more abundantly."* (John 10:10) In Romans 5:1 it says, *"We have peace with God through our Lord Jesus Christ."*

Everyone who wants to live forever with peace, having an abundant life, raise your hand.

Where we're at

So, just to be clear, our sins (our crimes against God) have separated us from Him. In that state, He does not listen to us.

Isaiah 59:2 says, *"But your iniquities have separated you from your God; your sins have hidden his face from you, so that he will not hear."* In God's book we

We get forgiven because Jesus came and paid our bill.

are dead since God said our sins require the death penalty (Romans 6:23). But, He made a way back for us through Jesus. While God is offering grace (a get-out-of-death free card), it doesn't come without a price. **The debt for our sins is real. The cost is death because sins have to be paid for. We get forgiven because Jesus came and paid our bill.** He paid with His blood when He died on the cross in our place. In YOUR place.

Remember when Jesus said, *"I am the way, the truth, and the life…?"* The rest of that verse continues, *"no one comes to the Father except through me."* He's making sure we understand that there is just one way to heaven, one way to be restored to a relationship with God. It's Him. Only Him.

1 Timothy 2:5 says, *"For there is one God and one mediator between God and men, the man Christ Jesus."* And 1 Peter 3:18 says, *"For Christ died for sins once for all, the righteous for the unrighteous, to bring you to God."* What Jesus did was to bring you to God.

Please read that last sentence again.

Why did Jesus die for you? **TO BRING YOU TO GOD.**

To restore you SO THAT you can stand in God's presence. SO THAT you could come to God, YOUR FATHER, and talk to Him. SO THAT God would listen. SO THAT you, yes YOU, could have a fresh start and do life from here on out with GOD.

Jesus DIED for us, to save us from missing out on that.

The really, really great news is that Jesus didn't stay dead. Jesus proved He was the authority over death when He rose from the dead. The Bible tells us Jesus fixed what Adam (man) had broken, *"For as in Adam all die, so in Christ all will be made alive."* (1 Corinthians 15:22)

In fact, our eternity starts right away. In John 5:24 Jesus says, *"I tell you the truth, those who listen to my message and believe in God who sent me have eternal life. They will never be condemned for their sins, but they have already passed from death into life."* (NLT)

Want to stop being dead?

If what Jesus is offering sounds pretty good, I've got even more good news for you in case you missed it. Salvation (being saved from death and hell, being made right with God, being made alive for all eternity) is a FREE gift. The only thing you have to do is BELIEVE that Jesus is the Son of God and that He came here in human form, that He died on the cross to pay for your sins, and that He rose from the dead.

Romans 10:9 says, *"If you declare with your mouth, 'Jesus is Lord,' and believe in your heart that God raised him from the dead, you will be saved."*

John 1:12 says, *"Yet to all who received him, to those who believed in his name, he gave the right to become children of God."* We not only get forgiven, we get adopted. God truly becomes our Father!

Look back at the door. Your door. Realistically, this is not the door to your room, but the door to your heart. The door to your life. Jesus is still out there, knocking. In Revelation 3:20, Jesus says, *"Here I am! I stand at the door and knock. If anyone hears my voice and opens the door, I will come in and eat with him, and he with me."*

Have you decided whether you want to let Him in? **Hold that thought for one more minute.** I'm not going to try to talk you INTO it, in fact, it might sound like the opposite. But that's how Jesus rolls.

Why people mess up at this point

Well-meaning Christians and many churches often push people to make this commitment and accept Christ. They will tell you to pray that you're sorry for your sins, say you believe Jesus died for you, and say that you commit your life to Him. In the name of Jesus, Amen. WAYYYY too often, people think it's the ritual that saves them. They believe if they pray a prayer using the "right" words, that statement makes them a Christian – earns them salvation. **It does not.**

As I mentioned in the beginning, this is a big deal. The biggest. It's not just saying something. It comes down to a BELIEF and a BIG, HUGE decision.

Of course, most people want to go to heaven, but saying you WANT to go to heaven does not GET you into heaven. What does?

God is saving you FROM sin and death TO something: A life with Him. Guess what? When you choose to do life with God, guess who's going to be in charge? (Hint: It's not you.)

Choosing to be saved from sin and death is not only believing Jesus can do that – it's saying you want the RESULT of that. Wanting to be with GOD forever is what you must be saying yes to. Wanting to be done running your own life and wanting God to be in charge of your life is what you have to say yes to. Wanting to follow Jesus the rest of your life, and not going your own way, or someone else's, is what you need to be saying yes to. Jesus came to get you to take you away from this dead life, and TO GOD so you can live – REALLY LIVE!

So what does this look like?

If you're ready to open the door to Jesus, you have to be done running your life the way you think is best. In Proverbs 14:12 King Solomon, (the wisest man who ever lived) said, *"There is a way that seems right to a man, but in the end it leads to death."* We think we know what would make us happy. What life we should have. **That thinking is dead wrong.**

Repenting is going toward God and away from sin.

If we are truly asking God to forgive our sins, to accept His Son's death as payment for those sins, then we have to be done with them. Luke 13:3 says, *"But unless you repent, you too will all perish."* The word repent means to change directions, primarily a change of mind. God is in the opposite direction of sin. You must be ready to leave your sins behind. **Repenting is going toward God and away from sin.**

If that sounds impossible, you just haven't hung out with Jesus yet. In the Bible Paul went through so much crazy stuff, yet he said, *"I can do all things through Him who strengthens me."* (Philippians 4:13 NASB) Jesus himself said, *"With people it is impossible, but not with God; for all things are possible with God."* (Mark 10:27 NASB)

Accepting Salvation is trusting that God has a better plan than us. It is to set out on a journey to follow Jesus, letting Him take us to God. It's allowing Him to show us how to live, how we need to change to be our true selves (that God planned for us to be), and how we live as His children to impact the world for His glory. It is embarking on a journey that will be hard at times, filled with wonders, and an adventure that will last for all eternity.

Is it time to open the door?

Just like any journey, you may still have a lot of questions but many cannot be answered unless you go. I'm not going to sugarcoat it. Jesus himself said, *"In this life, you will have trouble."* (John 16:33) What great adventure doesn't have ups and downs? Sometimes this journey gets seriously real and it's hard. A lot of that will happen because we need to change how we act, how we think, and how we relate to others. Each person will have baggage to unload, junk to deal with, and truths to embrace. But you will also experience freedom, grace, peace, and love like you've never imagined. So, are you ready?

Accepting Salvation, opening the door to Jesus, is the absolute beginning of life!

Another reason people mess up at this point is because they think Salvation is something you get and you're finished. **Accepting Salvation, opening the door to Jesus, is the absolute BEGINNING of life.**

How to open the door

You pray. That just means you talk to God. Stand up, or sit down, or get on your knees – whatever you feel moved to do. Close your eyes (or don't) and "see" yourself walk to the door. If you have decided you want to, open the door.

If you opened it, you see Jesus smiling. **Invite Him in. Talk to Him.** There's no formula for what you need to say – just talk to Him now that you know what He came for. It's actually good if you can talk out loud. Even though God can hear your thoughts, speaking or even whispering your conversation with Him is important. It gets us out of thinking mode and makes our decision an affirmative action.

What it comes down to is you believing that Jesus was sent by God to die for you, to restore your relationship with Him, and to help you get to God. Repent of your sins and give yourself to Jesus. Here's what you might pray:

> God, my life is a big mess. I've thought, said, and done a lot of things that were not good. I don't want to be like that anymore. I've been going the wrong way. I want to be part of your family. I want to be your child. I want to go YOUR way.
>
> I know that you sent your Son Jesus here to pay the penalty for MY sins, to die in MY place so that I can be with You from here on out. Thank you for making a way for me to be restored.
>
> I'm opening the door for Jesus to come in to show me how to do life now. I'll probably need a lot of help to get this right, so I'm counting on You. Help me to clearly understand how to hear Him and see Him so I can be who you created me to be. Thank you for loving me and saving me.
>
> Amen. (That just means "Yes.")

Take your time with Him. Talk to Him. Listen to Him.

When you're done, write down what you decided and what you experienced.

Day 3

GETTING TO KNOW JESUS

A GOOD POINT

Jesus was God and man in one person,
that God and man might be happy together again.
- George Whitefield

I'd love to know what went on between you and Jesus yesterday! I pray that you either gave your life to Christ or recommitted your life to Him. If not, if you are truly seeking some answers, what follows may be helpful. Realize that revelation of God's Word (that would be *The Holy Bible*) is for those who are honestly seeking Him. Your mind will be able to grasp only what God allows you to know. For those who are truly seeking Him and His will for their lives, the supernatural will occur when we draw close to Him and His Word, and we will be privy to many depths and insights. It is truly a remarkable experience that you will treasure.

For those of you who are taking the journey, Welcome! I'm so, so excited for you! If you are someone who has been on a journey with Jesus before yesterday, and are looking for a more meaningful relationship, this is a good day for you. If you are new to all of this then you'll be starting out strong!

We are going to learn how to KNOW and SEE Jesus. How to really be WITH Him. Having grown up in the church, no one ever told me how to have a relationship with Jesus that felt real. I didn't even know we were supposed to have a relationship with Him or that it was even possible. I missed out on so much for so long! Praise God I had a very dear person teach me how!

Extra credit. Look up these verses and note who Jesus is telling to follow Him.
You may need to read a few before and after each one to figure it out.

Matthew 16:24
Matthew 19:21
John 10:27

I learned this concept in the heat of battle and it has helped me, maybe more than anything else, to strengthen my relationship with Him. I still do it. I can't NOT do it. How's that for some bad grammar? But I bet you totally get what I'm saying. It's what takes me from *thinking* ABOUT Jesus to *being* WITH Jesus. Before we get into the how-to, we need to get a little knowledge under our belt about who this Jesus guy is and what we're supposed to do with Him. Why we need to spend time with Him.

Jesus said we were to both *believe* in Him and *follow* Him. What's the value in following someone – especially someone you spend time with day after day, year after year?

What do you think might happen to you? *Jot down some thoughts.*

You'd probably know them really well. You'd know their quirks, how they say things, what was important to them, what got them riled up, and what made them laugh. If it's someone you admire, that you want to be like, you may even find that you've picked up some of their attributes. Maybe you find you are more easy going, not prejudice like you used to be, find the value of pouring into others, see that being humble is not a weakness but a strength. Unfortunately, we can admire bad traits in a person if we see a benefit — like being rude and forceful equals getting your way.

A motivational speaker once said, *"You are the average of the five people you spend the most time with."* We become like the people we're doing life with. Think about the 5 people you have spent the most time with recently.

What can you see in them that is also showing up in you?

You are the average of the five people you spend the most time with.

-Jim Rohn

Who we spend time with is critical to who we are and who we'll become. Another popular quote says, *"Show me your friends and I'll show you your future."* If we want to be what God created us to be (filled with love, joy, peace, and purpose) it starts by following the example of His son and letting Him rub off on us. It actually goes deeper than that. Look up the following Bible verses and write down what is going to happen to us.

Romans 8:29: We will *"be ______________ to the image of his Son…"*

2 Corinthians 3:18: We are *"being ________________ into his image…"*

We are going to change so we are just like Jesus. We don't *become* Jesus 2.0, but we will become perfect like He is perfect. We'll have all the major character traits He has. We will think and act like He does. Nope, probably not happening overnight. It will be a process, but God says it will happen.

So, what is Jesus like? Look up the following verses and draw a line to the attribute of Jesus that is described.

Matthew 9:36	• Compassionate
Mark 10:45	• Eternal
Luke 23:34	• Willing to serve people
John 8:12	• Forgiving
John 15:9	• Humble
John 15:13	• Loving
Philippians 2:8	• Willing to sacrifice himself for his friends
1 Timothy 1:16	• A light to others
Hebrews 13:8	• Unchanging/solid
Revelation 1:8	• Patient

Read through the list of Jesus' attributes again. How would you feel about yourself if this list described you? Think about that for a moment.

This is just a short list that describes the person of Christ. He is so much more as you will discover. Jesus is the guy who likes kids and fishing and telling stories that make you lean in and think. He is bold and pushes people's buttons and even ticks them off — mainly because He always tells the truth. When that truth comes up against those who are unwilling to change, against our plans or expectations, we don't like that very much. The truth hurts as they say — or it can set us free.

What I've learned about Jesus is that you can always count on Him. He's ALWAYS going to be there. When you hang out with Jesus you'll realize He asks a LOT of questions. He has so much treasure, but He rarely brings you the chest of gold. Instead He takes you to the area it's in and gives you the experience (frustration and joy) of digging up the bounty. He is loving beyond measure, kind, patient, and firm. Sometimes He'll pick you up off the floor tenderly and sometimes He'll lovingly, yet sternly order you to, "Get up!" He knows when you need compassion and when you need a kick in the pants. He's funny. He's your friend and your most intimate partner. He knows everything and still believes in who you can be. He never, never, never gives up on you. Never.

One mistake I made about Jesus early on was the thought that He and Satan were about the same when it came to how much power they had. That was so ridiculously wrong! Look up the verses below and write down one more attribute of Jesus (or more accurately, write WHO Jesus is).

Colossians 1:15 & John 1:1 (Hint: The "Word" refers to Jesus)

I like how the NLT version of Colossians puts it, *"Jesus is the visible image of the invisible God."* Jesus IS God. He created the world, the universe and everything else. He is The Boss of everyone and everything. Satan has been defeated by Jesus. Therefore, we can count on Jesus as our protector and our fortress. Nothing is getting past Him. End of story.

I used to be so afraid that I would slip through the cracks somehow, be deemed not worthy, blow it one too many times and push Jesus away. That was complete lunacy. That might be how we've seen the world work. Jesus is not that. He is the One who stays, helps, guides, and protects.

Look up these two verses and write down what Jesus will do for us who believe and trust in Him.

Jude 1:24. *"to present you before his glorious presence ______________ ______________ and with great joy..."*

John 10:29. *"...;no one will _________ _________ out of my hand."*

Those verses changed my life. To know that I could be made perfect and that nothing could steal me away from God was everything to someone who figured it was just a matter of time before I messed it up for myself. Figured I already had.

Take another look at John 10:29.

Who can snatch you out of Jesus' hand?

Look again at Jude 24.

Who is going to keep you from stumbling? Who is going to present you without fault (perfect)?

No one can snatch you away. That includes YOU. If you want to be with God then God will make sure that happens. You can't mess it up. If you gave your life to Christ, then it's His job to keep you safe. Your part is to keep going His direction and leaning in. Like a runner racing for the goal, you win when you focus on the prize (Jesus) and lean in with all you've got (Christ's power) to break through the finish line.

Okay, so how does being with Jesus become a reality for you? Go back to John 10 one more time and read verses 1-16 then fill in the blanks.

"...his sheep follow him because they know ________ ____________. (v. 4)

"I am the good shepherd; I _________ my sheep and my sheep __________ me..." (v. 14)

Knowing Christ's voice and knowing HIM are what keep us safe in the flock. My husband's uncle was a master lamb producer for many years and he had a huge flock of sheep. We would call this modern day shepherd a sheep farmer. When the kids would visit they would try to get the sheep that were far off in the pasture to come over to the fence so they could give them handfuls of grain and pet them. They would call and whistle but the sheep just kept grazing. As soon as Uncle Bob stepped up to the fence and whistled, a thousand head of sheep snapped their attention toward the one who they knew and came a runnin.' That was the one that took care of them. That was the one they could trust. They knew who to listen to and they learned to ignore any counterfeits of that. We too need to learn Our Shepherd's voice and know Him well so we know when it's NOT Him. We get to know Him and His voice by sitting with Him. Literally sitting with Him. Being with Him.

Tomorrow we'll dive into HOW to do that well in a way that I pray will be as life-changing for you as it has been for me. For now, talk to God about what you've learned today and pray that He will continue to guide you and draw you closer and closer to Him.

Day 4

THE EXCHANGE

A GOOD POINT

I have been crucified with Christ and I no longer live,
but Christ lives in me. -Galatians 2:20

Yesterday we discovered some of the benefits of hanging out with Jesus. Being with Jesus is how we are going to get to know Him and how we'll be changed to be like Him. This is how we begin to let Him lead our lives. We listen and learn from Him — let Him rub off on us. This is the first big hurdle to living the life God wants for you. **The life YOU want for you.**

Let me explain that. Right now, you probably have a lot of ideas about what you think will make your life good and happy. Take a few minutes to jot them down.

What are your goals, dreams, and thoughts about what your best life looks like? Consider things like education, career, family, relationships, social life, hobbies, and how you want to be or feel.

If you're like most people, we think we need certain things, experiences, or relationships to make us happy. Most people believe things like romance, a thriving career, and financial stability will make us happy. Yep, for about five minutes. Then they will just be something we're used to and it won't be as fulfilling as it once was.

In the song, *Calling All Angels*, by Train, a line captures our appreciation for those achieved dreams perfectly, *"In a world that what we want is only what we want until it's ours."* In other words: **Satisfaction in worldly pleasures doesn't last.**

A former dentist of mine is a profound example. Dr. Tiedje grew up poor and watched his family struggle with money on a daily basis. He vowed he would never be poor when he grew up.

He studied hard, put himself through college, and became a dentist. Since money was what would make him happy and offer a problem-free life, he decided he was going to be a *great* dentist so he could make a great deal of money. He was, and he did. He married and had kids. He had a great family and they bought a spectacular home. The cherry on top was being able to pay for THE car of his dreams. He had it all.

Then why did he end up in his bathroom with a gun, contemplating suicide? He was supposed to be happy. He had achieved the all-American dream! Why did he feel so incredibly empty? He thought he knew what was best for him — what would make him happy. But it didn't last.

The good news is this story has a happy ending. The young Dr. Tiedje didn't pull the trigger. Instead, he went to his knees and cried out to God, *Was this all there was? Was this all that life offered?* He heard God whisper to his heart, *The reason you feel empty is because you are tying to fill a God-size void with worldly stuff. Only I can fill that place.*

He knew that all of his striving and acquiring hadn't worked, so he placed his life in God's hands and his life changed forever. He heard of a need in Africa and he knew God was sending him. He and his wife sold or gave away everything they had and moved their kids to begin their real life in Africa serving as dental missionaries. He and his family served in that role, fulfilled and joyful for many, many years.

Dr. T. thought he had a good plan. He didn't. He thought he'd find fulfillment and prove he'd made it when he had the keys to a certain kind of car. Jesus knew using Dr. T's abilities to serve others was the true key to success and fulfillment.

Okay, don't freak out! God's probably not going to send you to Africa to do your job. The point is, we will never find out what God has in store for us until we stop living OUR life. We won't feel complete. Nope, sorry *Jerry Maguire* movie, no thing or person outside of Jesus will ever make you feel complete.

So how do we stop thinking about what we want, what we have planned and start letting Jesus lead the way and reveal HIS plan? How do we let Him change us so we want what He wants?

As Jesus followers, we need to realize that something amazing took place when we asked Jesus to take over our lives. **When we accepted Jesus, a transaction took place. An exchange.** He took something from us and put something in its place.

Read the verses below and fill in the blanks.

Micah 7:19 says, *"You will trample our sins under your feet and throw them into the depths of the ocean!" -NLT.*

Psalms 103:12 says, *"He has removed our sins as far from us as the east is from the west."*

He took away _____ ________.

What did he give us? Acts 2:38 tells us, *"Peter replied, 'Repent and be baptized, every one of you, in the name of Jesus Christ for the forgiveness of your sins. And you will receive the gift of the Holy Spirit.'"*

He gave us ______ _______ __________.

Why did we get His Spirit in exchange for our sins? The Bible is pretty clear. On our own we WILL mess up our relationship with God. God sent Jesus to save us, to show us how to live, and when Jesus was getting ready to leave he told his disciples not to worry. *"And I will ask the Father, and he will give you another advocate to help you and be with you forever; the Spirit of truth...he lives with you and will be in you."* (John 14:16-17)

When Jesus was resurrected and went to be with God in heaven, God sent the Holy Spirit, Christ's Spirit, to not only be *with* us as believers, but to take up residence *inside* us. In Galatians 2:20 it says, *"I have been crucified with Christ and I no longer live, but Christ lives in me."* Remember, Jesus said He will be with you always (Matthew 28:20) and He sent His Spirit to be in us (John 14:16-17).That means He is with you now. With His Spirit inside you, you will find it's not hard to talk to Jesus and be with Him "in spirit." It's not as weird or mystical as it may sound.

Perhaps you've joked with a friend who had to do something uncomfortable (like having a colonoscopy) and you quipped, *"I'll be with you in spirit!"* You weren't really there. *Your* spirit can't go anywhere your body isn't. But Jesus' Spirit can. When Jesus is with us "in Spirit" He is really, fully with us so we can hear Him and communicate with Him. When people say they "hear" God tell them things, most often this is what they mean. They don't hear an audible voice, they hear Him in their spirit, in the voice that does not always require words. You'll just KNOW it was Him.

We are not human beings having a spiritual experience. We are spiritual beings having a human experience.

-Pierre Teilhard de Chardin
Theologian, philosopher, paleontologist, geologist.

Tuning into that just requires us to tune into our own spirit. Think about it, you are you because of the thoughts you think, the way you feel, and how you make life work from the inside out – from your spirit. That's where all the important stuff happens. In fact, Pierre Teilhard de Chardin said, *"We are not human beings having a spiritual experience. We are spiritual beings having a human experience."* If this seems a little confusing, don't worry, it will all make more sense when you start experiencing it.

It's time to pull up a chair

Here's how to be WITH Jesus so you know He hears you and that you hear Him: Pull up a chair. Literally. Find a spot for Jesus to sit close to you. Now, look at Him as you talk to Him. It's good if you can talk out loud so it feels more like a conversation and less like thoughts. It's okay if you need to whisper. As much as you can, remind yourself that Jesus is with you: in the car, at work, at church, in jail, when a telemarketer calls, when your kids are acting their age, when your spouse is being unreasonable, when you don't know what to do, Jesus will be right there. Find a spot for Jesus and give it a try.

For starters, tell Him what you like best about Him so far. Then, tell Him what you like best about yourself.

When I started doing this I realized I thought about Jesus so much more. At first it was mostly in the morning when I took time to read my Bible and pray before I started my day. It was just the two of us and that time became so precious to me. I started understanding things I hadn't understood before. Things that used to seem so important and required so much of my time faded away. Things that really mattered came into sharp clarity.

And no, it wasn't all goodness. I had to hear hard things about myself. But I didn't have to *deal* with it by myself. God does something inside of us that enables us to change — even things that we've maybe tried a bazillion times to rectify on our own. So, in the end, it was all good.

As we read yesterday, you will begin to recognize His voice when you hear it — and you may hear it in many places. I have heard Him in movie dialogue, a friend's advice, a pastor's sermon, an inspiring song, and in warm sunshine while in McDonald's drive-thru. I can't even tell you how many times I have felt Jesus' presence, guidance, intervention, revelation, comfort, and love. It never gets old. It is the most satisfying, fulfilling thing in the world. I tell Him everything. He is the best counselor you'll ever have! With Him, everything you need will be provided and you'll realize a bunch of stuff you thought you needed you just don't.

After some years of being with Jesus everyday — "seeing" Him, I had it in mind to ask Him a question that wasn't answered in the Bible. Something I would ask any friend. I asked Him which animal was His favorite. He created all of them after all — surely there was one He was especially proud of. I instantly thought of a tiger. It wouldn't be my choice (I'd say an elephant), but I wanted to make sure I didn't just think that because I'd recently seen a program on tigers or something. Nothing came to mind. A moment later I KNEW why He said tigers and I literally cried as I remembered.

A few years earlier, when I was in the hardest time of my life, I was so afraid that God had given up on me, so afraid of God's judgment of me. God led me to a book that spoke of how we can trust God's promises and that He is there not to harm us but to bring us comfort. One of the most compelling passages in the book was the analogy the author made to God. She compared God to a tiger and posed the question: Who does not need to fear the tiger? Answer: tiger cubs. That gave me such peace in that moment and was a treasured image that reminded me that I was a beloved child of God. All these years later, I'd nearly forgotten how significant that was to me. God hadn't.

I have been crucified with Christ and I no longer live, but Christ lives in me. The life I now live in the body, I live by faith in the Son of God, who loved me and gave himself for me.
Galatians 2:20

Sit with Jesus. Talk to God

Your relationship with Jesus can be so intimate and personal. Right now, lean in and talk to Him. Tell Him everything and ask Him to help you hear Him. Let Jesus share your life, drive your life, and you'll find your best life.

Day 5

WHY THIS WILL WORK

A GOOD POINT

A healthy person has a thousand wishes
but a sick person only has one. - Indian proverb

You can't be in the presence of God without changing.

Our title for today may seem like a strange one. The word THIS doesn't imply *this study* it means, why a RELATIONSHIP with Jesus will change your life…REALLY change your life. The answer is pretty simple: You can't be in the presence of God without changing. You will be very uncomfortable if you are with Him and resistant to change. In fact, you won't be able to stay there if you have no intention of transforming. He won't leave you, you will leave Him.

That sounds super discouraging so let's decide right here and now that when things get uncomfortable we will know it's a sign that something has to change. That *we* have to change. YOU will need to change. That's kind of the whole point so let's promise ourselves to lean in and not run off. Being uncomfortable only lasts until we decide to believe God and do things His way. Learning to do that as soon as His way is presented can take some time, but it's so refreshing when you start figuring it out. In the coming weeks, we're going to get into HOW to let God transform us. HOW to get through and past the hard stuff, the discomfort, and get our own wills and self-made roadblocks out of the way.

For our last day together this week, I want to encourage you and tell you that learning how to KNOW God really will change everything in your life. I know it first hand and I know many others who do as well. What I thought would NEVER be fixed is not even a blip on the radar of my life anymore. The thing that CONSUMED my life, including nearly every thought, for far too many years, and stole my joy is GONE.

It's interesting, because at one point I was in a place that I felt I could *cope*. That may be the worst four letter word there is. Coping is standing on a tightrope, a fault-line, a house of cards. If nothing shifts you'll be okay. But things don't stand still for long. God quickly sent someone to rattle my world. It was so ridiculous – I was actually annoyed with that person for wrecking my shaky hope. Coping is a lie where we tell ourselves we'll be fine. *"Just don't think about it." "Avoid that at all costs!" "Don't…" "Make sure…" "If I just…"* It's an impossible, stressful way to live.

With God, He loves us too much to leave us even a little broken. He is the God of wholeness — The Restorer, The Redeemer. I don't care if you've tried to change, stop, or fix something in your life before. You may have even prayed about it. This is different. This time it's going to get personal.

When I was in high school, I liked the band Aerosmith. I bought an album — once. When my son was in high school, he too liked Aerosmith. So much so that he bought their CDs, signed up to be in their fan club, went to their concerts, and even got their band logo tattooed on his back! (Kids don't always listen to their mother.) Guess what? If Steven Tyler (the lead singer) ran into either of us we'd be super excited, but he wouldn't have a clue who we were. I think we have a similar idea about Jesus. The Bible even covers it. Look up Matthew 7:21-23 then answer the question below.

Who were the people Jesus was talking about? People who...

- [ ] didn't believe in Him
- [ ] weren't active in the church
- [ ] did things in His name
- [ ] didn't worship Him

Those who do things in His name are just like the fan of a music band. We may do all kinds of things that, from our end, look impressive, yet we don't REALLY know The One that's the leader. To put it in a modern context, Jesus is saying, *"You do all this stuff at your church, you sign up for service projects, and give to some charities, but you don't KNOW me. Just because you sing my name in a few songs doesn't mean we're close. I don't even know you."* Ouch.

This is one HUGE reason most people do not have a life-changing relationship with God: They DO things for God instead of BEING with Him to get to know Him. If you get personal, this will work. God works.

So, let's recap our journey this week a bit. *First,* God gets that many of us show up as a big, hot mess on this road with Him. God's grace isn't limited to WHAT we've done. It's available to us when we realize we need help — help that only He can give. *Second*, we understand that Jesus is the only way to get us to where we are going. He has restored our relationship with God, our Father, and He will take us to Heaven to be with Him forever. *In the meantime,* He's here to show us how to live, change, and fulfill our purpose while we're here. He'll transform us from our lives of mediocrity, hangups, wounds, and sin and transform us to be like Him — into who God has planned for us to be: filled with peace, love, and joy. *Finally,* we began sitting with Jesus. We learned how to be with Him, to make this relationship real and personal. We'll continue getting into that deeper in the coming weeks.

For now, go back and re-read A GOOD POINT at the beginning of today's lesson. Think about that and write what you think it means in the margin.

If you are going through some deep waters right now, maybe even an actual sickness, you probably figured out what the saying is getting at. When things are good, you think about all kinds of things. When things are bad, that's all you can think about.

Change only happens when the pain of staying the same is greater than that of changing.

There's a saying, *"Change only happens when the pain of staying the same is greater than that of changing."* Maybe the word "only" is a little strong, but the word "usually" would probably be accurate. For those of you who really, really need something to change, I'm not all that worried about you completing this study. You will probably stick it out because you ARE more afraid of nothing changing than of what something new and different means. You know what your "one wish" is.

Do you know what your "one wish" is?

If you aren't going through a hard time, I'm a little more concerned about you. Why? We only make time in our lives for things we deem as valuable to us. It's so easy in this nation of abundance (abundant entertainment, food, opportunities, etc.), to CHOOSE something that will take up our precious resource of time. Most people won't choose to spend time with God if they don't have to. That's a terrible thing to say, but it is so incredibly true and I can't imagine how much that breaks God's heart. Most of us only go to God intimately or intentionally when we are in trouble. If you don't feel like you're in trouble, many of us give God a little passing nod now and again, and that's about it. *"Hey God, thanks for the great dinner! You're the best. Later!"*

I truly don't say that to try to guilt you. I say it to encourage you and applaud you if, in fact, you are being moved in some way to draw closer to Him. If you don't feel a desire to be with Him, please hear me tell you, that can change.

It can be a scary thing to realize that you don't love God. That you don't want to hang out with Him as much as doing something else. Please don't worry if that feeling isn't there just yet. If you are willing to show up each day and just tell God you need Him to help you love Him, to give you a desire to be with Him, to want to want the things He wants (say that 10x fast!), it will happen.

Mark on the *Love Meter* below where you feel you're at with God right now.

I have three "keys" let's call them, to developing this relationship with God. They aren't rules, just advice. Remember, this IS NOT a program or a process to be proficient at. It is how you do life with THE ONE who will be the greatest love of your life. Take it as you would marriage advice.

The 3 Cs of relationship with God

1) Commitment: **Set aside time to be with God everyday.**

If you just got married, no one would need to tell you to spend time with your spouse. You would WANT to do it. It would only make sense that you'd find time to be with someone you signed on to share your life with. And, you'd know that they'd want to be with you too. Let's face it, showing up is probably the biggest way to prove we are "all in" with any relationship.

> **HOW:** Six days a week we'll be here to guide you and give you stuff to talk about with Him. On "off" days, ask Him what His plans are for you. Thank Him for the good stuff (there's always good stuff) and talk about the hard stuff.

2) Consistency: **Read something from the Bible each day.**

Someone once said, *"Praying is how we talk to God. Reading the Bible is how God talks to us."* Our communication with God needs to be a two-way street. Often our relationship with God is like we're on a trip and we send postcards to our Loved One. We are the only one sharing about our journey and we wait until we get home to find out anything about them. Jesus is on this trip with us. In fact, He's leading us. We need to know what He has to say.

> **HOW:** Again, six days we'll get you into the Bible. On any open days, read a chapter or two. Ask God to help you understand it and how it applies to you. If you're brand new to Bible reading, start in the New Testament. The book of Luke gives a good overview of Jesus' life in a straightforward way.

3) Communication: **Make sure you're sharing.**

Sit with Jesus and tell Him EVERYTHING. You'll be amazed how much better you feel. Don't fall into the trap of holding back. When we start feeling a little better about a hard situation we tend to convince ourselves we don't need to go deep — *"It will get better...just wait."* Or, when an old wound flares up again we ignore it, push it down. Meanwhile it's eating away at our peace, ousting our joy. The more we open up to God about ALL that is happening, the sooner He will speak to us about how to deal with those issues — once and for all. Nothing is too big or too small to share with The One who loves you unfailingly.

> **HOW:** Each day when you're with God, share your day. What are some things that made you smile? What are you worried about for someone else? What's bugging you personally? Get real. Ask God to help you understand how to handle things. Think about what you read in the Bible and how it might apply to what's going on in your life. Just be real.

Sit with Jesus. Talk to God

Go through the 3-Cs with God. 1) Set a time and place you'll meet each day.
2) Get a Bible if you don't have one (see pg. 148 for help).
3) Tell God something meaningful you want Him to know.

The single biggest problem in communication is the illusion that it has taken place.

-George Bernard Shaw

Satisfy us in the morning with your unfailing love, that we may sing for joy and be glad all our days.
Psalm 90:14

Do the wrap up at the end of your week — perhaps on your Day 6. It's a good way to recap what you've learned all week and capture the things that were most important to you.

Time For A Change

WEEKLY WRAP UP

Write what point, quote, or Scripture stood out most to you this week

This week's memorization verse

I have been crucified with Christ and I no longer live, but Christ lives in me. The life I now live in the body, I live by faith in the Son of God, who loved me and gave himself for me.
Galatians 2:20

Hey! I hope you had an amazing start or restart this week! I'm wondering about you right now. I'm wondering how your week in this study went and whether you're feeling hopeful or overwhelmed. Excited or confused. One of the reasons I decided to write this study was that when I went looking for answers to my deepest struggle and hurt, and inevitably just how to LIVE out this life of faith in Christ, much of the information people gave me was full of "Christianese." You know, those words or phrases that Christians use that only they understand. Things like, *"Let go and let God,"* or *"Lay it at the foot of the cross."* Truth is, they couldn't really explain HOW you'd do those things. I know I gave you a lot of information this week, and I pray it made sense. Just in case, let me clarify a couple of things.

I think the two most important points this week that are critical for having a life that is FULL in every way — the way God intended — are these:

First, realize that a life with God, through Jesus, is a TRANSFORMED life. If God is going to live IN us we have to have a fit place for Him to dwell. If you don't think you need to change, you are very wrong. If you don't want to change, you might as well close the book and walk away. God is Holy (set apart) and so we have to be as well. We can't look like everybody else — we have to start looking like Jesus. We have to want to be different. While that can seem daunting, don't worry, we'll catch on as we follow Him, sit with Him, watch Him, and listen to Him.

That idea scares most of us. Changing. We fear things we are not in control of. You may not believe me just yet, but hear me tell you — what you think you want is only that way because you don't know what Jesus has in mind yet. Once you get to know Him better, you will see that His way is the only way. Not only will you understand that, you will find peace and freedom in His way. Truly.

Second, BEING with Jesus (sitting, driving, or walking with Him) is crucial. Some might say that I've got a screw loose — conjuring up an image of Jesus next to me. Talking to "it." Scripture is clear, Jesus said He was never going to leave us. Yes, He is here in Spirit — not physically, and NO, it isn't the same. I want to hug the physical person of Jesus so much! While, I'll have to wait until heaven for that, I am embracing the reality of Him in the way that is possible. By talking to Jesus as if He *were* in the flesh, I keep Him REAL to me. He doesn't become a far-off God. I never think of Him as away or uninvolved. What really validated His presence with me was when I realized **I NEVER imagined Him. I just started acknowledging that He was already in the room.** Do you sense Him in your room as well? If so, don't pretend He's not.

Accepting Christ is HUGE. Now, the biggest factor is learning to be WITH Jesus. I cannot stress that enough! Everywhere you want to go in life, be, and do is wrapped up in knowing Him. He has to be real to you. As you start the process of following Him, I will tell you, it will be hard at times but it becomes so much easier when you sit down and talk to Him about everything – even if you're mad, ticked off, confused, or unsure. This is where everything begins to change.

Taking stock: Answer the questions below to process this week's study.

What were some key things that you felt Jesus nudging you about this week?

What was the most positive thing you felt Jesus wanted you to hear this week?

Sit with Jesus. Talk to God

Turn your answers above into a prayer. For example, if I wrote that I felt Jesus was nudging me about not wanting to change some things and I really felt like I am forgiven I might pray, *"Father, I am so happy that you forgive me – even when I have trouble forgiving myself. It gives me hope that things can be different. When we were studying about changing to be like Jesus I know I doubted I could ever be that good – and part of me didn't want to change. Please help me want what you want. I'm going to need lots of help. In the name of Jesus I pray, Amen."*

Knowing Jesus Tip:

Protecting some time each day when just you and Jesus hang out is essential. The more consistent that time is (number of days and time each day) the more likely you'll do it. About 10 years ago, when I realized I was not going to make it without Him, and knew if I didn't stay close to Him I'd wind up right back where I was (and I NEVER want to go there again), I started making time for us. For me, I give an hour to do some Bible study (something like this) and literally talk to God about EVERYTHING. I had to get up earlier each day to make that happen, but it is one thing I have never regretted, nor felt was a chore. What I get out of it is such a blessing —it's life to me.

WEEK 2

PLANT YOUR FEET

If you have ever surfed you know in order to ride the waves, you've got to have a good stance on your board. Same goes for skiing. Your boots had better be securely anchored in your skis in order to maneuver through the snow like a pro. Without that bond between feet and foundation you are going to crash.

Our homes, our businesses, our relationships too all need a firm foundation. If not, it's only a matter of time before things fall apart. Our journey of faith is no different. We have to know what core beliefs and truths we have under our feet in order to stand firm. You don't start building a house until you've got the foundation poured. That's what we are doing this week. We're finding a place to stand that will be solid if things get shaky down the road.

Just an FYI: If you've ever learned to surf or ski, you know you fell down a lot while you were learning. You are likely to have some wipe outs in your faith — especially when some big waves come — when you don't see that rock under the snow. Just like being proficient at those sports, the basics are the same. If you fall down, get back up (on your skis, board, or faith foundation) and try again. You only fail when you quit getting back on.

Photo: Alex Iby, Unsplash.com

Day 1

HAVE SOME FAITH

A GOOD POINT

Believe your beliefs and doubt your doubts.

-F. F. Bosworth

How easy is it for you to go on faith? Are you someone who is pretty trusting, believes the best going in, or, are you leary from the start, expecting that someone is going to fail you? Maybe somewhere in between? For those who trust pretty easily, what I'm going to suggest won't be a hard sell. For those closer to the other end of the spectrum, we'll need to chat.

As Christians, we gave our lives away in faith. We chose to die to ourselves – believing there really, truly is someone better suited than us to run our lives. I know full well that some have entered here on very *shaky* faith. You've been disappointed too many times. People you should have been able to trust have let you down. For some, it's a sheer miracle that you are willing to try one more time. I don't take that lightly.

A few years ago, writing for a magazine, I wrote a feature telling some stories of people who had gone through *Adult & Teen Challenge*. If you don't know what they do, they are a Christian-based residential and rehab program for those trapped in addiction and life-controlling issues.

For the article, we had former *Adult & Teen Challenge* students who submitted their stories. They told about their past and how they wound up in addiction, about their experience in the program, and how they are doing today. These were some amazing, life-changing stories! With the beginnings and experiences they endured, it was easy to see why many of them turned to mind-numbing options. Real life was way too much to bear. There were a couple of tales so terrible I had my hand over my mouth as I read them. Some made me cry. I realize for some, asking you to have faith is a scary prospect.

With that in mind, I pray you'll hear me on this: If you don't go in expecting something good, it's likely you won't find it. Expectation can set the stage for the kind of experience you'll have. Want to have a good experience – expect one. Expect to have a bad experience – you've set the bar.

> If you don't go in expecting something good, it's likely you won't find it.

We want to go in prepared for the best so let's find a few key things that are going to help us on the rest of the journey. We need to build these as our default setting to help realign us if we get confused, scared, or start doubting.

We are going to experience those things on our journey, I can pretty much guarantee it. Putting a few truths under our feet now, in faith, will help us stand strong when we come up against difficult issues around the corner.

Nope, this isn't blind faith. It's taking God at His word on a few things now. Pitching our tent on solid ground and deciding that we won't move when things down the road seem uncertain, upsetting, or we don't understand. We'll remember our foundation, and work from there.

In the coming days we're going to grab three strong pillars of truth. With Jesus as our capstone, we'll set our supports under His feet. Today, we need to start by understanding what it means to have faith.

Merriam-Webster Dictionary

Faith: To believe that (someone or something) deserves to be trusted.

Look up the verse below and fill in the blanks.

What is faith according to the Bible?

"Now faith is ____________ in what we hope for and __________ about what we do not see." -Hebrews 11:1

The writer of Hebrews is talking about faith in God. Feeling assured and confident in what we're hoping is true, even though we can't see everything at the moment. The NASB version says, *"Now faith is the certainty of things hoped for, a proof of things not seen."*

Typically, if people have a life-verse or favorite Bible story, it's because it hits close to home. When I was going through a crisis of faith, Jesus' simple words in Mark 5:36 comforted me: *"Don't be afraid; just believe."*

Overhearing what they said, Jesus told him, "Don't be afraid; just believe."
Mark 5:36

Now Jesus' words aren't just some nice platitude for everyday life. Let's check out what's going on.

Read Mark 5: 21-43. When Jesus told the man not to be afraid, but to believe in Him, what had happened to the man's daughter? (v. 35)

When I needed to hear those comforting words of Christ, I was struggling to believe that God could forgive me. That there was any hope for me. What I heard God say was, *"No matter how bad things are, no matter what it looks like from an earthly perspective, no matter what you're hearing from others, just trust ME. I will take care of everything. Don't be afraid, just believe."*

I realized that once we belong to Jesus we are not our own. God's got this. This revelation gave me such peace. So much so that I even journaled about the experience. As I was writing it all down back then, just before Christmas, another serious thought hit me.

A few weeks before, in early December, no one could find my niece. She had struggled with depression and addiction for several years. We phoned everyone we could think of trying to find her. A couple of days passed, yet she was still unaccounted for. The police were called, the family rallied, and we searched. A week later, police found her body, curled up in an inconspicuous area, just a few yards from a shopping mall. A stark contrast to the hustle and bustle of the lively holiday shopping around her. An accidental overdose had ended her young life.

As I journaled about trusting Jesus instead of looking at circumstances, the desperate father from the Bible verse took on my sister's face. She too had asked for a miracle from God. Where was *her* daughter's healing? This is what I felt God telling me and what I wrote in my journal that December day:

> It can't be ignored: Jasmine died. Why didn't Jesus save her? I believe He did. When she was rehabbing for those two months before her death she spent time reading her Bible. I believe this was God's plan to have time with her – to show her who He was – so she was His. Jesus did save Jas – He took her home with Him.

The answers to our prayers will often not look anything like we imagined. Sometimes all the evidence points against the good. But circumstances and feelings aren't the whole story.

Through my own crisis of faith, I took my fears and struggles to God. He showed up time and time again. But we forget that we can count on Him. Especially when things get hard. That's when I decided to start a journal. I entitled it, "*When God Shows Up.*" It is filled with experiences I had that were undeniable God intervention, revelation, and conversations...and I didn't record even a fraction of what happened. Just the biggies.

What I know is that we just have to hang in there long enough to get the answers. There will be a moment when you hear the right message, read the right scripture, get reminded of a truth, and suddenly your doubts melt away. One by one, over and over, having faith, sticking it out with Jesus and believing the best, He will deliver.

Faith is not the absence of all doubt. It's continuing to follow Jesus while you figure it out.

Often people think doubt is a lack of faith. Nope. Faith isn't the absence of all doubt. It's continuing to follow Jesus while you figure it out. Doubt can even be a good thing. Doubt means you're not taking everybody else's word for it. People get themselves in trouble when they just automatically believe what mom and dad or granny had to say on the matter. We have to own OUR faith

OURSELVES. It's okay to question things.

The one person you DO need to believe though is Jesus. He will help you through any faith struggles, but you need to believe what He says (which you'll find in the Bible).

Evangelist F.F. Bosworth said, *"Believe your beliefs and doubt your doubts."* In other words, don't start thinking what you believe is wrong just because you have some doubts now and again. Don't consider trading truths for lies and assumptions. Hang in there, take those doubts to God with the expectation that He will sort things out for you. Hang on to what you have. That's how you build your faith — keeping what faith you have and tackling the next obstacle will expand your faith and make you stronger.

Have faith that Jesus is always with you. Always.

...surely I am with you always, to the very end of the age..
Matthew 28:20

Sit with Jesus . Talk to God

Just like last week, find a spot for Jesus to sit (if you haven't already invited Him in). Even if you find this really awkward yet, you need to push past that discomfort. It isn't you IMAGINING Jesus, it's you giving space to the REALITY of Jesus' promise that He would always be with you (Matt. 28:20).

His Spirit is with you so embrace that truth and talk to Him. Look up the verses below and ask Jesus to help you believe these truths even when your circumstances don't seem to line up. Look at Jesus and hear the words as they are for YOU. After each one, write down what stood out most to you and tell Jesus why.

Deuteronomy 31:8

Psalm 23:4

Psalm 46:1

Matthew 5:4

John 16:33

Romans 8:37-39

Tell Jesus where your faith is right now. Let Him know if you've got some concerns, doubts, or struggles. Ask Him to keep you strong as you wait for answers and to not jump to conclusions. If you feel like your faith is strong, ask Him to reveal areas of weakness — ones you may not realize at all.

Thank God that you can have faith in Him and that His word says we don't have to worry, but that we can put our trust in Him (Mark 5:36).

Day 2

LET'S HAVE A WORD

A GOOD POINT

Faith is daring the soul to go farther than it can see.
-William Newton Clark

Today we're going to grab onto our first pillar of truth we'll need to own. To start, in the margin, write down what you believe right now about the Bible.

How you see the Bible will greatly impact your ability to have a deep relationship with God. Let's dig in and see if you can put your first foundation stone in place.

Foundation pillar #1: Believe the Bible is true.

Look up the verses below and fill in the blanks.

2 Timothy 3:16. Where does scripture come from?
"All scripture is ________ -______________..."

Proverbs 30:5. What will God's word prove to be?
"Every word of God ________ _____________;"

Isaiah 40:8. How long is God's word good for?
"...,but the word of our God ________ ___________."

If the Bible is really from God, "The WORD of God," without error, and was written to be applicable forever then why aren't we hanging on every word?

We know if we believe the Bible we will have to change.

Today, much of the world will try to convince us that the Bible is not accurate, is not to be trusted, is outdated, and full of contradictions. I wonder if our protests come down to a more simple issue: We know that if we believe the Bible we will have to change. We don't want to live the way God wants us to. At least we don't think we do.

Years ago, before I started really wanting to know what God wanted me to know, I was honestly afraid of the Bible. I figured it was just full of stuff that I would never want to do and probably wouldn't be able to get myself to do. I think I was going with the "ignorance of the law" excuse. Like standing before God saying, *"But, I didn't know,"* would fly when He knows I've got that Bible they gave me when I graduated into second grade Sunday School *and* the one that my grandma gave me when I was 16 with my name engraved on it. The one that I gushed over as I opened it while internally rolling my eyes. The one that was still in the box.

Saying we didn't know isn't going to cut it.

When I really started diving in, REALLY wanted to understand, there were parts that absolutely scared me, parts I just didn't understand, parts that confused me, and stuff I questioned, stuff I doubted...a lot. Then I heard something about the famous evangelist and pastor Billy Graham that changed my mind. His grandson, Will Graham, tells the tale:

> At the mid-point of the 20th century, he had already been an evangelist with Youth For Christ and had preached across Europe in the aftermath of World War II. He had held his first "Billy Graham Crusades"... He was also the president of Northwestern College in St. Paul, MN.
>
> Not everything had gone as planned, however. His crusade in Altoona, PA, had been – in his own words – "a flop." It was spiritually difficult and he felt things had gone poorly, and it left him questioning whether or not evangelism should be his focus.
>
> At the same time, a very good friend and contemporary of my grandfather's, a man named Charles Templeton, had begun challenging my granddaddy's way of thinking. Mr. Templeton, who had preached with Youth For Christ as well, had gone on to study at Princeton, where he began to believe that the Bible was flawed and that academia – not Jesus – was the answer to life's problems. He tried to convince my grandfather that his way of thinking was outdated and the Bible couldn't be trusted.
>
> My grandfather had more questions than answers.
>
> As a young man in his early-30s, all of these things were swirling in his mind when he traveled to California in 1949. Should he invest fully in the college...which would require taking several years off from preaching, should he leave and follow the calling of an evangelist, even though Altoona had gone so poorly?
>
> Did he even believe the Bible from which he was preaching, or should he follow Templeton in questioning its validity?

"Thus sayeth the Lord."

> It was at this time that my discouraged grandfather reluctantly accepted the invitation to visit and speak at a Christian retreat center, Forest Home. While he was there, he spent a great deal of time studying the Bible, and he kept seeing the same phrase pop up. *"Thus sayeth the Lord… Thus sayeth the Lord…"* While my grandfather had always accepted in his head the authority of the Scripture, this became the turning point as he realized in his heart that God's Word is divinely

> inspired, eternal and powerful!
>
> One night at Forest Home, he walked out into the woods and set his Bible on a stump – more an altar than a pulpit – and he cried out: "O God! There are many things in this book I do not understand. There are many problems with it for which I have no solution. There are many seeming contradictions. There are some areas in it that do not seem to correlate with modern science. I can't answer some of the philosophical and psychological questions Chuck and others are raising."
>
> And then, my grandfather fell to his knees and the Holy Spirit moved in him as he said, "Father, I am going to accept this as Thy Word—by faith! I'm going to allow faith to go beyond my intellectual questions and doubts, and I will believe this to be Your inspired Word!"

Father, I am going to accept this as Thy Word—by faith! I'm going to allow faith to go beyond my intellectual questions and doubts, and I will believe this to be Your inspired Word!

-Billy Graham

In a book that Charles Templeton later wrote, he told about how their debate about the Bible ended:

> Finally, Billy said, "I've discovered something in my ministry: When I take the Bible literally, when I proclaim it as the word of God, my preaching has power. When I stand on the platform and say, 'God says,' or 'The Bible says,' the Holy Spirit uses me. There are results. Wiser men than you or I have been arguing questions like this for centuries. I don't have the time or the intellect to examine all sides of the theological dispute, so I've decided once for all to stop questioning and accept the Bible as God's word."

Unfortunately, Charles spent his life as an atheist. In an interview at the age of 80, he sobbed after revealing that he missed Jesus.

Billy Graham's decision to live a life of faith, believing that the word of God was without error, speaks for itself as he opened up the truths of God to multi-millions of people. He himself led a full and wonderful life.

We all have to make the same decision. Here, there is no halfway. That's how God is. We have to believe all of it because saying we believe some of it is calling God a liar. Remember, in 2 Timothy 3:16 it says ALL scripture is God-breathed.

After I read the article about Billy Graham, I too decided to take a stand and say I believe it 100% — by faith. I figure that if God is God then He can certainly get what He wants into the Bible EXACTLY how He wants it — despite what man has to do with it.

Over the years, I've gotten stuck, gotten scared, and been confused plenty of times. I absolutely do not understand everything, and I won't. Not in this lifetime. But, what I have learned is that everything I NEED to understand for my journey, for my purpose in life, God has given me understanding. The way that God has made the Bible come alive for me and revealed things I never saw before is one of the big ways I KNOW that God is real. It has been supernatural. When that started to happen, I got so excited! It became like a drug. I just wanted more and more. It's an experience you don't want to miss.

Sit with Jesus. Talk to God

Yesterday we grabbed onto the fact that **Jesus is always with us**. So, once again, let's make sure we're fully aware of His presence. If you haven't already done it, ask Jesus to take His seat near you again. Say Hi. Get comfortable. Tell Him about a couple of things that made your day (today or yesterday). Now, ask Him to help you to understand that you can have faith that His Word, the Bible, is trustworthy. Go through the following exercises with Him.

2 Timothy 3:16-17

The word of God is good for:

Read 2 Timothy 3:16 again and continue through verse 17. In the margin, jot down all the things that the word of God is good for.

Read Ephesians 6: 10-17. What does the verse describe God's word as?
"...the ______________ of the Spirit, which is the word of God." (v.17)

Circle what that word conveys about the Bible.

Tool Weapon Faith Test

We'll come back to Ephesians 6 in a moment, but first read Matthew 4: 1-11. How did Jesus use it as a weapon against the devil?

Go back to Ephesians 6. Why were we to put on the full armor of God?
"...so that you can take your stand against _______ ____________ ____________" (v.11).

Who is our struggle with? (v.12). ________________________________
____

The reality is, we need the Bible. We need its instruction, guidance, correction, power, and protection. To believe in the Bible, fully and completely, is to have access to God's arsenal of knowledge and power to fight against all that the evil forces will try to defeat us with.

Are you ready to take a stand today and accept God at His word that His Word is true, reliable, and a means to guide you and protect you? Talk to Jesus about it and tell Him your decision, then write it below.

Day 3

THE REAL GOD

A GOOD POINT

Faith is deliberate confidence in the character of God
whose ways you cannot understand at the time.
-Oswald Chambers

Today, revel in the fact that you are walking with the two most powerful forces in the universe – Jesus and His Word! Let's start by getting Jesus into position, aware that you are letting Him guide you today. Reach out and shake His hand – unless you'd rather give Him a hug. Ask Him to help you truly feel His presence today and to give you insight into our lesson.

Foundation pillar #2: Believe God is __________.
Look up the verses below and, in the margin, jot down the adjectives used to describe God. Find the common descriptor to fill in the blank above.

Psalm 100:4-5	1 Chronicles 16:34
Psalm 34:8	Mark 10:18

From the Old Testament to the New Testament, those who knew God knew that He was good. ALL good.

In 1 John 1:5, Jesus says, *"This is the message we have heard from him and declare to you: God is light; in him there is no darkness at all."* God's not good *sometimes* or when *things* are good, but He IS good. He can't be anything BUT good.

God is light; in him there is no darkness at all.
1 John 1:5

James 1:17 agrees with that thought, *"Every good gift and every perfect gift is from above, and comes down from the Father of lights, with whom there is no variation or shadow of turning."* You can count on God being good. All the time. Every time.

Let me tell you about Kelly. Kelly likes to swim, loves fish, and the sight of guns makes Kelly very nervous. Based on that limited information you start developing a picture of Kelly in your mind. One might imagine Kelly is a fitness fanatic, health-conscious, and she had a traumatic experience as a victim of gun violence. Or, you might see Kelly as a boat owner spending weekends with his grandkids, fishing, and pulling off on a sandbar for a dip to cool off. Someone who writes letters to his governor petitioning for tighter gun laws. However you imagined Kelly is likely wrong because Kelly is a duck.

If we imagine God to be anything but who God actually, fully is, then we are not worshiping the true God, but one we've created in our mind. And that version is fictional. God is who God is. He can't be anything but that.

For those who have had a pretty easy life, believing God is good isn't a stretch. But what if you have suffered loss? Loss of a job, trust, a relationship, dreams, health, a child?

What if you prayed for your marriage to be restored but the divorce happened anyway? What if you prayed for healing but the sickness lingers? What if you prayed for protection for your teenager but they became an addict? When hard things abound, God can seem anything but good.

Yet, circumstances don't change the facts. If God being good is a fact AND our struggle is a fact then how do we reconcile those things? What if in our current location, we just can't see the whole picture?

A few years ago, my pastor gave an illustration: Imagine life as a parade with Jesus leading the way. When we are toward the back of the parade, we can't see what's around the next corner, or the next. But God knows because He's already there.

What if instead of thinking God isn't good, isn't listening, doesn't care, etc., what if we thought, *Because God is good, and this hard thing is in my life, there must be a valuable purpose for this. I will trust in God's goodness. I will stay close to Him for comfort and direction.*

We won't *always* get an answer for everything that comes our way, but we can expect to have *peace* about everything. Look up Psalm 27:13

When did David believe he would see God's goodness?

We may have to wait until we get to heaven to get the full insight, but God will provide what we need now to feel okay about things.

One frequently quoted verse about God's goodness is Roman's 8:28. *"And we know that in all things God works for the good of those who love him, who have been called according to his purpose."*

Reread that verse and answer this question:

If we are in a loving relationship with God, what things is He going to work out for our good?

For some of us, our struggle in accepting that God is good is perhaps our idea of what good means. Maybe we need to define what is good.

How would you define goodness? Jot some thoughts in the margin.

Would you say cancer is good? Most people would give that thought a resounding, "NO!" One man I interviewed for a magazine article a couple of years ago would have a different answer. I want you to hear some of what he experienced so you can appreciate his perspective.

> Phil had a bad cough that just wouldn't go away, and his neck and shoulders seemed to be getting thinner, so he got a physical. During the exam, the doctor poked his belly and told him to relax. That *was* relaxed he told the doc. Phil had written off his bulging waistline as an inevitable 40-something beer gut. The doctor said, "This isn't good." Tests ensued to reveal a very large tumor.
>
> Big decisions had to be made and too many options and obstacles made those decisions seem impossible. Many people had lots of advice, but it was during a song at church that Phil got some clarity. God spoke to Phil in the line, *We won't move without You.* Phil choked back the tears as he remembered, "I realized I was literally not supposed to do anything. I had been praying for answers and now it was as if someone was saying, *'Don't do anything.'* And I'm thinking, *Really, seriously? Come on, I have to do something.* And it was as if God was saying (not verbally, but clearly), *"I'll take care of this, you just don't do anything.'"*
>
> Phil said, "I felt like it was a fantastic resetting for me. It was a before and after experience. Everything before was bad and scary and confusing, and everything after was okay."
>
> But Phil's wife wasn't so sure. What were they waiting for? Phil didn't know. He just waited on God. A couple of weeks later, Phil heard God say, *"Go."* They went. Events pointed them in the direction of the Mayo Clinic and even though there should have been no way that they were able to get in when they did, an opening occurred at just the time they could arrive. Another unexpected opening allowed them to get an important test they needed immediately. They diagnosed Phil's condition and made a plan to remove Phil's 30-pound tumor.
>
> The surgery was a success. However, for this type of cancer, it's unusual for it NOT to come back. As Phil got close to his first checkup, he wasn't worried that the cancer had returned. Instead, he was afraid that everything would be fine.
>
> Phil explained, "I pretty much stopped praying to have God take it away. I really started praying for other things – to have this be a good thing and not a bad thing, to be thankful for what He has done." But Phil's biggest worry was about losing something priceless he'd gained.

It was a before and after experience. Everything before was bad and scary and confusing, and everything after was okay.

> "I felt I could go and talk to God and he would talk back to me. In that moment, my one big prayer was for God to keep me in that eternal perspective I had gained."

Cancer was really the best thing that ever happened to me.

> Phil went on to say, "Cancer was really the best thing that ever happened to me. It was the hardest thing — but it was the best thing. I got to a point where it was a clear choice: I could either live like I was going to die and be dead forever, or I could live as if I was going to live forever, regardless of how long my life was. And I lived that way, and it was fantastic."

Based on my story or Phil's, I would say goodness is whatever it takes for us to wind up with God. But then, God tapped me on the shoulder and reminded me that there are people who have endured horrific things. I have cried for you as I thought about those in sex trafficking who have endured some of the worst atrocities. There are soldiers and others who have experienced terrible things. Things that are not and never will be deemed as good. So what is good?

Good is a God who draws us toward Him, to open our eyes to our deep need for Him, resulting in us accepting His son and surrendering everything to grab onto that salvation with everything we have. Good is a God who will take all of those terrible things and reshape them so we can live at peace with them by taking all their power away from our lives. **Good is what God will do with your life to make sure you are saved and made whole.**

God is good — not because he causes things that seem or feel good to happen in our lives, but because in the midst of the storm, God comes closer to us than the storm could ever be.

–Charles Spurgeon

We are going to have hard things in our lives — and the people we love will too. It doesn't mean God isn't good. In fact, it could be the exact opposite. In his commentary on Psalm 46, Charles Spurgeon wrote that *God is good — not because he causes things that seem or feel good to happen in our lives, but because in the midst of the storm, God comes closer to us than the storm could ever be.*

Sit with Jesus. Talk to God

Read Psalm 46 with God and talk to Him about being able to trust in His goodness. If you are going through a hard time, ask Him about trusting that He has something good in mind. Pray about the thought of not asking God to stop the hard season, but that you learn and grow and are blessed by it.

Today, don't forget to focus on what goodness God is providing in your life now. Even in the hardest times there are golden nuggets of truth, insights, and blessings in disguise. Some may be glaringly obvious. Thank Him.

Are you ready to accept that God is good and own this pillar of your faith foundation? Tell Him what you decide then write it below.

Day 4

THE GREATEST

A GOOD POINT

Faith is not the belief that God will do what you want.
It is the belief that God will do what is right.
-Max Lucado

Today we're grabbing the last of our foundational pillars. Having faith that Jesus is our only way to God (our Savior), the Bible is God's Word (without error), and belief that God is good (always) will carry us far — and our last pillar is no less important.

Are you ready to dive in? You are if you've invited Jesus to not only sit with you but to be the one leading you. Take a moment and settle in with Him. Ask Him to help you see Him...even what He is wearing. Share a little about what's going on with you.

Like yesterday, let's start by defining what our foundation pillar is.

Foundation pillar #3: Believe God is __________.

Look up the verses below and, in the margin, jot down the adjectives used to describe God. Find the common descriptor to fill in the blank above.

Psalm 86:15
Isaiah 54:10
Romans 5:8
1 John 4:7-8

1 John 4:8 says it all: God is love. Just like God IS good, God IS love. Of course He is loving, but also, God is the source of love. He is the embodiment of love.

Love is one of those words that can get thrown around a little too loosely so, for some, it may seem less important than it is. Others rarely or never hear it so you may have a much different idea.

What do you think it means to love? Jot some thoughts in the margin.

Let's take a look at what the Bible says about it — and more importantly, how God shows His love. As you may have guessed, love is one of those complex emotions that puts its arms around some significant real estate. It takes in a lot of territory — and rightly so. Those who we are in love relationships with are the most impactful, meaningful, and life-altering. When we can begin to understand God's love for us we can feel secure and grounded.

1. God's love is sacrificial. Take a look at a couple of the most important verses you will ever read.

Read John 15:13. What is the greatest way to show love?

Read John 3:16. What did God sacrifice for you and what do you get out of it?

Think about who you would die for? Likely, only someone you love greatly. Now who would you sacrifice your *child* for? Anybody on your list? God did the unthinkable for YOU.

2. God's love is unshakable. Isaiah 54:10 says, *"'Though the mountains be shaken and the hills be removed, yet my unfailing love for you will not be shaken nor my covenant of peace be removed,' says the Lord, who has compassion on you."* Do you understand what this is saying? If you have given your life to Christ, basically, no matter what happens, what comes down the line, what you do or don't do, God is still going to love you. Always.

Okay, I'm going to put a little disclaimer in here for the ones who are thinking, *"You can't just do what you want!"* That is true...but sometimes we do what we *don't* want to do. Other times, we are still learning what those things are we shouldn't be part of. If we are truly children of God, Jesus followers who want to be better, believing that HE has done everything that needed doing to save us, there is no limit on the amount of times He will forgive us. Past, present, and future, Jesus has it covered for us. No matter how long we keep messing up, however long it takes us to be transformed, as long as we are leaning in, repenting, and learning from our Savior, we're good. The problem lies with those who *say* they are following Jesus but just use that as a license to sin. If we are truly walking with Jesus it will bother us greatly to sin.

3. God's love is eternal. Look up Romans 8:38-39 and fill in the blank.

What does it say can separate us from God's love?

"For I am convinced that neither death nor life, neither angels nor demons, neither the present nor the future, nor any powers, neither height nor depth, _____ _____________ else in all creation, will be able to separate us from the love of God that is in Christ Jesus our Lord."

One of the things I had to realize is that I, myself, fall into the "not anything" category. Please hear me on this. For those of you who think you have done too much wrong, keep messing up, never seem to get it right, God put this verse in there for you! YOU cannot mess this up. It's not up to you. His love for you is so powerful that NOTHING, including you, is going to change that.

I think God gave me grandkids to begin to appreciate how He loves us. I can't even tell you how much we love our grandkids...it's beyond measure! I would die for my grandkids. Our grandson Jack is autistic. That means Jack can be a handful, frustrating, and disobedient at times. When he was a toddler, he could not be expected to do anything *for* me, yet, it didn't change how I felt about him. I just love him no matter what he does or doesn't do. Nothing could ever change that. That's how God's love is for us.

Read 1 Chronicles 16:34 and fill in the rest of the scripture that tells how long God will love us, *"Give thanks to the Lord, for He is good; His love endures ____________."*

Always. Forever. Not until the last time you sinned. Not until that huge, unforgettable no-no. Not until anything. Say it out loud: His love endures forever.

4. God's love is just. Want to know what the Old Testament is about? It's hundreds of years of story after story about how God kept coming after us in love. Go back and look at the Good Point quote at the beginning of today's lesson and fill in the blank.

> Faith is not the belief that God will do what you want.
>
> It is the belief that God will do what is __________.

Love does not mean enabling our bad behavior. A loving parent disciplines their child. Why? So the child learns how to live in a way that benefits society as well as provides for a peaceful, joyful, and secure life of the child as they grow into adults. Often, troubled youth and adults plagued with struggles, come from homes with little or no discipline.

Over and over in the Old Testament, God tells people how to live in order to please Him which would result in many blessings and benefits. He is clear that NOT doing those things would result in negative outcomes in their lives. Of course, we humans think we know better, and we put it to the test. After all, doing things OUR way just might get us what WE want, when WE want it. God lets us go for awhile on our own and then He sets things in motion to get our attention. When we've tried to touch the hot stove a dozen times even though we're told over and over not to, eventually we're going to have to get burned to learn why we shouldn't. While our God is a loving one, He loves us enough to get our full attention when we're doing wrong and He will do whatever is necessary for us to stop our bad behavior.

God loves us enough to get our full attention when we're doing wrong.

George*, a married man, struggled with lust and was operating in inappropriate ways. He knew he needed help, but was ashamed to tell anyone what he was dealing with — he was a church-going man after all. He prayed

*Name changed.

that God would help him to stop. When his wife walked in on him that prayer was answered, but not in the way George imagined. People found out. His wife's trust in him and his reputation were destroyed and it took years to rebuild his life. God answered his prayer in a way that struck the killing blow to his sinful life, yet George was mad at God. He just wanted those desires to go away. Why did it all have to be out in the open? Because God isn't a genie to grant our wishes. He is a loving God and a just God. He didn't let George betray his wife and pretend like it never happened. By exposing it to the full light of day, George was forced to deal with the issue, which led to the realization that there were MANY issues that played into this secret sin that George was ignoring. That the couple were ignoring. Because God did what was right, the man grew stronger, his marriage was healed and strengthened, George has compassion for others who struggle in similar ways, and he has a deeper walk with God, secure that God will guide him and protect him — sometimes from himself.

5. God's love is transforming. In Week 1, Day 3 we explored this idea. See if you can fill in the two scriptures we covered then from memory.
Romans 8:29: *"For those God foreknew he also predestined to be ___________ to the image of his Son..."*
2 Corinthians 3:18: *"We all, who with unveiled faces contemplate the Lord's glory, are being ___________ into his image with ever-increasing glory..."*

In 2013, *Time* did an intensive investigation of who the *"100 Most Significant Figures in History"* were. According to the article they, *"evaluated each person by aggregating millions of traces of opinions into a computational data-centric analysis."* Sounds impressive! Guess who came out on top? Yep, Jesus.

Regardless of your religious affiliation, Jesus impacted and transformed the world in big ways and is still doing that today. We can see that Jesus is different. He was bold, unafraid, focused, a great friend, a leader, humble, compassionate, respected, made all the right decisions, and He honored God. Believe it or not, God is transforming us to be just like Him.

And now these three remain: faith, hope and love. But the greatest of these is love.
1 Corinthians 13:13

Sit with Jesus. Talk to God

God's love for us is manifested in many ways. Read 1 Corinthians 13:1-13 and feel God's love for you. Talk to Him about your thoughts about love in the past with people and what you are thinking about what God is saying in the Bible about how He loves — and specifically about how He loves YOU.

Tomorrow, you'll be the focus as we complete our foundation of faith. If your study time and place aren't private, this is a good day to get away by yourself.

Day 5

CHASING VICTORY

A GOOD POINT

Too often Christians have sought Jesus as Savior
but ignored him as deliverer.
-Beth Moore

Today is an important day because we are finishing off our foundation built on faith. This will be the solid ground we stand on as we go deeper and deeper with God, getting to know Jesus, and finding out how we live now in this new, transformed life. This is also a biggie because instead of focusing on God, we're turning the tables and have to look at ourselves.

As I mentioned at the end of yesterday's session, if you can, find somewhere private and quiet where you can be real with God. Don't be afraid of this, but be prepared to go deep. No "Sunday School answers" — you know, the ones you think are the right ones that will make everyone feel comfortable. Let's be radical and prepare ourselves to get uncomfortable if need be so we actually accomplish something meaningful. Know that I have been in your shoes and I didn't always like how it felt going in, but know too, that on the other side is relief and even some downright peace. Are you with me?

I want you to take a moment and talk to Jesus. Reach across and take His hands (see Him in your mind as you physically reach out), and pray something like this (aloud if you can): *Father, I know that part of this relationship is up to me. Let me hear with open ears what you want me to hear today. As I consider the questions, please let me be honest with myself and with You. Help me say what my struggle really is — mainly so I can hear it. You already know what the problem is. Let me not be too proud, or too scared, to admit it all. If I am not aware of something I'm doing that is not good for me or our relationship, please help me see it. In the saving name of Jesus I pray, Amen.*

Let me just be blunt: You are the problem.

I was the problem in my relationship with God too and it took me a good long while to stop being the problem…or at least be less of a problem. If you want your life to truly be transformed by God, to have the life He planned for you, the one that you will wish you had searched for soooo much sooner, the one without baggage, and pain, and doubt, and fear, then you have to get out of the way as fast as you can. What does that mean?

You have to believe in who you ARE and you have to tear down the lies about who you AREN'T. You have to believe EVERYTHING God says, do ALL that He tells you to do, and KNOW that there is more for you to learn.

Let's start with a few lies. First, check which of these may apply to you. Then, for those you checked, look up the verse shown and write down why that thought is a lie. I've done the first one for you as an example.

I doubt I will ever... **Why that's a lie:**

- ☐ be truly happy. God says I will have complete joy if I keep His commands. John 15:10-11
- ☐ feel unafraid. ______ Isaiah 43: 1-3
- ☐ feel deeply loved. ______ 1 John 4: 9-12
- ☐ have complete peace.______ Isaiah 32:17
- ☐ be free from worry. ______ Philippians 4:6-7
- ☐ feel good about myself.______ 1 Peter 2:9
- ☐ feel confident. ______ Joshua 1:9
- ☐ forgive myself.______ 2 Corinthians 5:17-19
- ☐ overcome my issues. ______ Psalm 55:18
- ☐ believe God really loves me as much as He loves Jesus. __ John 17:25-26

Okay, let's be real. As you marked the boxes and read the corresponding verse were there any that you read and had a *"yeah, but..."* thought? You know, "Yeah, but when I marked *I doubt I will ever feel deeply loved* I was thinking about [insert love interest here]. What this verse is talking about isn't romantic love." We have to stop thinking we know the answers to fix our lives. That reaction says, *"If I don't have a [significant other] in my life I'll never feel fully loved."* We need to focus on what God is saying. Perhaps when God's love is made complete in you you'll decide you really don't feel that drive to find a spouse anymore or perhaps you'll find that the romantic relationship God has planned for you appears – or, if you're already married, your marriage blossoms.

> Therefore, if anyone is in Christ, the new creation has come: The old has gone, the new is here!
> **2 Corinthians 5:17**

Another, *"yeah, but..."* may be, "Yeah, but I marked *I doubt I will ever feel good about myself* because the stuff I've done is beyond terrible! Now, I'm supposed to think I'm royalty! This is NOT talking about me!" Remember how 2 Corinthians 5:17 said you are a new creation? The old you is gone so you have to stop thinking you're what you used to be. You have to start believing what you are NOW. Yes, royalty.

My daughter will be the first to tell you that when she was in her 20s she made a lot of bad choices. A lot. Those choices led to years of drinking and using drugs. There was lying to loved ones. She was arrested more than once. She was raped. Her first boyfriend was murdered by drug dealers. Another boyfriend put her in the hospital, yet she went back to him over and over. Finally, she'd had enough. In church one Sunday, she fought against all the darkness that was keeping her down and she stood up and accepted Jesus. God rescued her and her life began to change. A few years later she wrote her story to help others who have gone down a dark path. A few things she said made so much sense for those struggling to believe in their new life.

> [When I gave my life to Christ] I literally felt a weight lift off of me. So much peace came over me as I prayed to God to save me from this life I was living. Being saved was my first stepping stone. One thing you need to realize is we don't change overnight. When I was saved, God let me step out of the darkness and into the light, but the darkness was so much of what I knew that it took some time to learn how to live in the light.

The darkness was so much of what I knew that it took some time to learn how to live in the light.

Jess aligns with what the Apostle Paul (who Jesus radically changed) said in Philippians 3:12b-13, *"...but I press on to possess that perfection for which Christ Jesus first possessed me. No, dear brothers and sisters, I have not achieved it, but I focus on this one thing: Forgetting the past and looking forward to what lies ahead," (NLT).*

My daughter stopped looking at the past, and focused on her future. Today, she has a happy life with a wonderful husband, who only God could have picked for her, and three beautiful kids. Her life has been completely transformed. She is one of the best people I know.

In coming weeks we'll get into the How-To of defeating our lies and putting our pasts behind us. For now, sit with Jesus and write down a couple of negative beliefs (aka: LIES) you have about yourself that bother you the most.

What negative beliefs are you most struggling with? Don't rush this. Ask Jesus to help you define them clearly.

The big key to defeating lies is with truth. We need to start replacing those lies and "used to be's" with current reality and define who we are now. For those of us who have accepted Christ, God tells us who we are. Look up the following verses and fill in the blanks below.

John 1:12	I am a ______________ of God.
John 15:15	Jesus calls me his ___________.
Romans 8:1	I am not ___________________.
Colossians 1:13	I have been transfered to _____________________.
2 Timothy 1:7	I have a spirit of _______ and _______ and _______.

How does reading that list make you feel?

If we are ever going to be who God made us to be we have to tear down the lies and dismantle walls of wrong thinking and start agreeing with God as to who we are and how we can live now.

As I was talking with Jesus about what our foundation of belief needs to include He revealed something so profound, yet so simple. This belief must be at the core of our foundation in order for it to be solid. The Good News that God sent His Son Jesus to deliver us comes down to three simple words: "God wants me." Say it out loud then write it below.

Foundation base: The Gospel: God ____________ _______.

Until we accept that absolute fact, our foundation will be shaky. Everything God has done is because He wants us to be with Him. Say it again, *"God wants me!"* As a statement of faith, write it in **My Faith Foundation** below.

While the road ahead may be bumpy as you chase victory with Christ, the foundation of truth you've started will serve you well as long as you remember to stand on it – seeing The One who is right there with you.

Sit with Jesus.
Talk to God
Review the foundation you've built this week with Jesus. Ask Him to give you all the truth you need to dismantle the lies you've identified, to be able to stand firm on these basic truths of who He is, who you are (loved and wanted by God), and that His word is true.

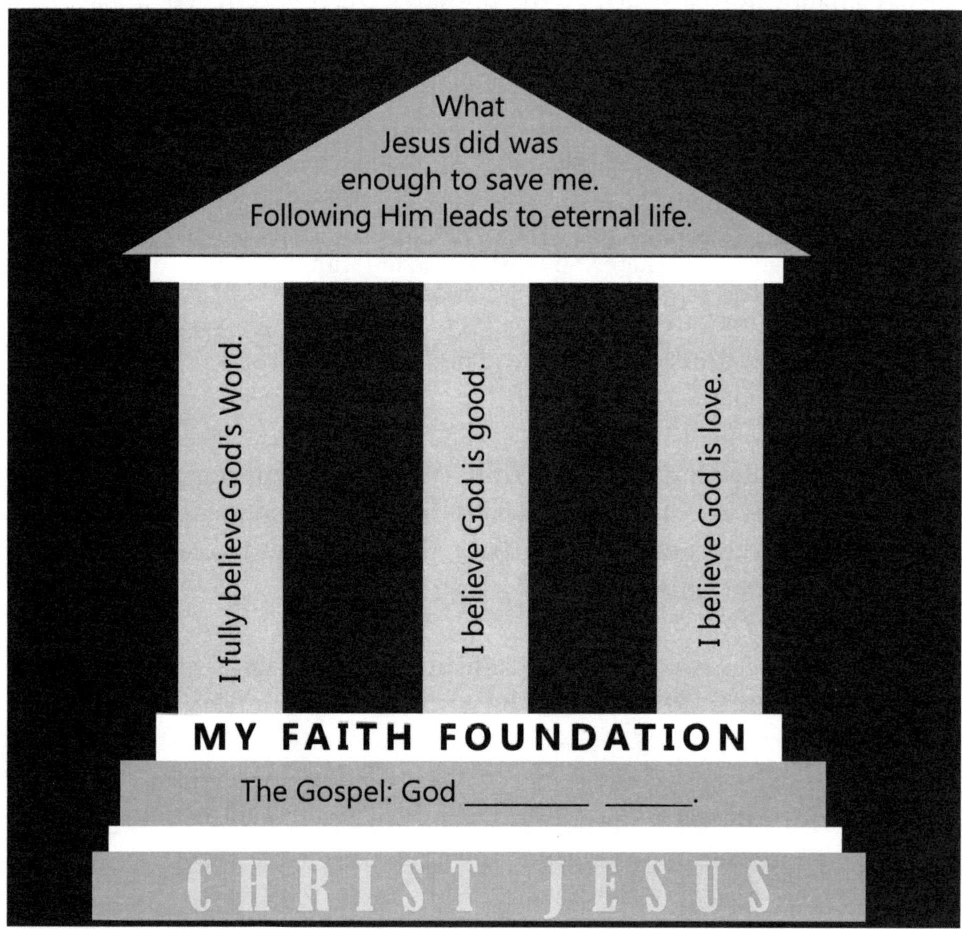

Plant Your Feet

WEEKLY WRAP UP

Do the wrap up at the end of your week — perhaps on your Day 6. It's a good way to recap what you've learned all week and capture the things that were most important to you.

Write what point, quote, or Scripture stood out most to you this week

Hey! I pray you can feel the solid foundation under your feet. As someone who thought they had a rock-solid faith, only to realize it was made of rubble when my world shattered, I understand it can be hard to trust. Hard to believe that God is truly good, loving, and trustworthy. In my hardest moment, I knew I had to start somewhere. **These were the truths I started with:** I WOULD believe God is good. I WOULD believe God is love. I WOULD believe that EVERYTHING the Bible said is from God. I WOULD believe that Jesus did enough to save me. I WOULD believe that God wanted me.

For some of you, that last thought may not be an issue. I'm wondering if instead you need that piece of your foundation to say **God is FOR ME**. It's the same basis. God is all about bringing His best plan for our lives — for us to be with Him.

Believe me, I wavered in some of those foundational truths from time to time. Life puts them to the test. Yet, I knew if I didn't stand firm on those, my life was truly going to crumble. Instead of abandoning my foundation, I just pressed in with God more. I expected answers to the seeming contradictions to these truths. Time after time God showed up and gave me insight and understanding. As I read the Bible and "meditated" on passages that stood out to me, I heard God.

Let me clarify that. I don't hear God with my ears, I hear Him in my spirit — in my mind, in my heart. He "reveals" things to me instead of speaks. It's Him connecting the dots — putting the puzzle together. You start to see what wasn't obvious before. You understand.

Let me also explain what I mean by meditate. Other "spiritual" practices make a big deal out of meditating so it can be misunderstood. You don't sit and say scripture over and over mindlessly. Meditating is actually a biblical word. Look up Joshua 1:8 and see the importance of it and what benefits are associated. Basically, meditating on Scripture just means you intentionally think about it. Roll it around in your mind throughout your day.

This week's memorization verse

Don't be afraid; just believe.
Mark 5:36

Knowing Jesus Tip: Keep tabs on what you think about in terms of God and your relationship with Him. If you start doubting and letting negative thoughts run away without bringing them to Him, you risk allowing them to undermine your life and faith. We act like we think — even if the thought is just a possibility and not proven — so don't let unexplored thinking get you responding in ways that can topple your foundation.

Simply pushing back against doubts and standing firm while you spend time with Jesus is a big deal. Often, when something strange or negative happens in our lives we can give up in the face of it. This is way too important to quit. Instead, press in with those questions to Jesus and get them resolved. In the book of John, Jesus told a large group of his followers something that baffled them and many of them walked away. He asked His 12 disciples if they would leave Him too. Peter said, *"Lord, to whom shall we go? You have the words of eternal life."* (John 6:68)

The ones who knew Him best were the ones who knew it would end up just fine. They just exercised a little faith.

Taking stock: Answer the questions below to process this week's study.

What were some key things that you felt Jesus nudging you about this week?

What was the most positive thing you felt Jesus wanted you to hear this week?

Sit with Jesus. Talk to God

Just like last week, whatever you wrote above is a great start of what you need to be talking to God about. Sit with Jesus and process through how you're feeling. Putting those thoughts into a prayer to God helps you start the process of working on some foundational faith elements.

WEEK 3

THE STUFF IN YOUR WAY

Have you ever thought a problem or situation was insurmountable only to find out later that it wasn't that big of a deal? Or perhaps the opposite has been realized — that something that appeared to be nothing ended up being like a mountain in your path?

This week, we're going to learn how to look at some of the things that can trip us up on our faith journey — on our getting to where we want to be journey — to the whole, happy, and at peace journey. To do that, we are going to begin to question EVERYTHING.

Right now, there are things in your way that you have just accepted. It's how they are. Maybe it's always been that way. It's what you've been told. It's what "they" say. It's your belief based on past history so it feels true. No more. We are going to listen to what God says and get some stuff out of our way. We'll pick up a couple of weapons along the way to help clear the road. Our road toward healing, confidence, and being as joyful as we should be doing life with The King of Kings!

Photo: Nathan Dumlao . Unsplash.com

Day 1
YOUR ASSUMPTIONS

A GOOD POINT

"God designed humans to observe our own thoughts, catch those that are bad, and get rid of them."
-Dr. Caroline Leaf

What we believe about just about anything comes from a lifetime of experiences, information, education, and influences. Some of that is good and some not so much. Sometimes we figure out which is which, but other times we may have assumed something is good or accurate when it absolutely isn't, and vise-versa. Since we made the decision that we're following Jesus, we've got to make sure our belief system is aligned with His — and weed out when it's not.

As I wrote that, I sensed the Holy Spirit nudge me to tell you that He does not expect you to blindly accept His ways. Our God is a big God and He is eager to hear all your questions. Even if they sound like protests and accusations initially. He loves you and is happy to guide you to the information and insights you'll need to see WHY His way is His way. Remember, if we are transforming to be Christ-like, that means our thoughts will be like His. It won't be robotic regurgitation of His thoughts. It will be YOUR thoughts as well. God will explain and open your eyes to His "whys."

If we're going to start understanding God's ways, we've got to know where we are at. This week we are going to question a lot of beliefs and assumptions, but today we're starting with what we believe about God. Last week we started to put together some information about God — that He is good and that He is love. If you are one who didn't already think that about Him, you may still be processing it and trying to truly believe those characteristics about Him. Sit with Jesus and tell Him what you really think about God in this moment. It's okay to be totally honest. Jot down your thoughts.

What do you believe about God?

I remember reading an article where someone described God as *"a mean kid with a magnifying glass looking for ants to burn."* You've probably heard the idea that God is a judge with a big white beard and a gavel ready to pronounce judgment against us. Some view God as a cosmic Santa Claus. If you've been good, you might get what you ask Him for. Realistically, what you believe about God may very well come down to your relationship with your earthly father. One daughter shares her experience.

> My dad never knew his father. His mom and grandma raised him. As a kid, my dad was a hard worker and was gone many evenings as well as working his day job. He was never mean, or harsh. My dad wasn't a hugger or one to say, "I love you." He always joked around. You know, the dad that says stuff like, *"Go play in the street,"* or when you're in high school headed out with your friends he might quip, *"Don't waste your dime calling me if you get arrested."* He was a likable guy and knew many people. When I was little, we sometimes visited some friends of my parents. They had two sons and when we would get ready to leave, their dad always said, *"You can leave that one if you want. We don't have any girls."* My dad would kid, *"Well, maybe next time."* What I realized over the course of my early years is that all that "kidding," with no verbalization that I was loved, left me with the following belief: *I think if I did something really bad my dad wouldn't want me. I'm not that important to him.*

That daughter is me. I didn't realize I even had that thought about my dad for decades. But, when I thought I'd done the unforgivable in God's eyes, I realized my belief of God was: *I did something really bad and now my Father doesn't want me. Ever. I'm not that important to him.* A few years later, after uncovering who God REALLY is and how He TRULY feels about me, I discovered the source of my insecurities. It all went back to my dad.

What I'm happy to report is that I was wrong on both counts, but you can see how we can put human qualities, experiences, and influences on God He doesn't deserve. We have to know who HE is and not what we BELIEVE Him to be.

Take a few minutes and review your answer about what you believe about God. Is there any connection between what you think and your past experiences with your earthly father — or other influential people in your life?

Can you give any insight into why you think what you think about God?

Way back in the beginning of the Old Testament is the story of God sending Moses to rescue the Israelites from slavery and the clutches of Pharaoh. They see God send the seven plagues against the Egyptians (including the invasion of flies and frogs and the river Nile turning to blood), ending with the death of every first born male child (while the Israelites sons were spared). Next, they leave only to be pursued by Pharaoh's army. God splits the Red Sea and they cross on dry ground — Pharaoh's charioteers are swallowed up and drowned. They follow God through the wilderness, seeing Him as a pillar of smoke by day and a pillar of fire by night. God feeds them manna (heavenly bread) that miraculously appears each day, more quail than they've ever seen, and when they're in the middle of nowhere He gives them water from a rock. Given this history with God, you'd think they'd trust Him with everything — unwaveringly. Sometimes, we are dorks.

God was leading them through the wilderness to take them to *"the promised land."* He told them it was, *"a land flowing with milk and honey."* He said there were people already living there but He was going to conquer them so they didn't need to worry. God told them to send 12 guys to go check it out. Read Numbers 13:26-33 then answer the questions.

Did they report more good things or bad?

Why did the majority doubt they could conquer the inhabitants? (Who were the occupants stronger than?) (v.31)

What did the Israelites see themselves as in comparison to the people there? (v.33)

Read Numbers 14: 1-4.

What did the Israelites assume God's motives were?

Turn back for a moment to Exodus 3:17.

What did God PROMISE to do?

Only do not rebel against the Lord. And do not be afraid of the people of the land, because we will devour them. Their protection is gone, but the Lord is with us. Do not be afraid of them.
Numbers 14:9

Our past experiences sometimes override our present realities. Even though the Israelites had seen God's goodness, they didn't believe it. They kept imagining the worst. Continue reading the story in Numbers 14: 5-10.

Who are the only two of the 12 who have a good report? (v.6)

What were the two things they said the people needed to do to succeed? (v.9)

What did the people want to do to Caleb and Joshua? (v.10)

Instead of being hopeful like Caleb and Joshua, they defaulted to their past history of treatment: People out to get them, take advantage of them, abuse them. Unfortunately, the people continued living in their fear and they never got to the promised land. They died in the desert feeling persecuted by God instead of loved by Him — their children were the ones who got what they had cried out to God for. He had rescued them from one hardship but they would not allow Him to deliver them to something better. Instead, they grew fearful and bitter, never feeling truly rescued. They assigned Him a character

He didn't earn or deserve. Everything went south for them because of two wrong assumptions:

1. WE will have to fight the giants in our way.
2. God doesn't really care about us.

Until we realize that God is for us and not against us, we too will wander in a wilderness of our own making. If we size ourselves up against our enemies, our problems, our hard things, and see ourselves as grasshoppers, this is where we feel like a victim. What Caleb and Joshua saw was that it doesn't matter what WE are. As writer Hannah W. Smith puts it, "*The question is not, whether we are grasshoppers, but whether God is; for it is not we who have to fight these giants, but God.*"

The question is not, whether we are grasshoppers, but whether God is; for it is not we who have to fight these giants, but God.

-Hannah W. Smith

Is there or has there been a situation where you felt like a grasshopper up against a giant?

When we believe we have to fight our own giants we will fail. We have to get to the place where we trust this God who has rescued us. That He is good, and loving, and that He will fight our battles and deliver us to a better place. A place that is wonderful. A place only He can take us to...after He destroys all that is in the way of our peace. Let's make sure we let Him.

Sit with Jesus. Talk to God

Did you remember to bring Jesus along with you today? As you sit with Him, talk to Him about what you believe about God. Ask God to help you see when you are assigning negative characteristics and assumptions to Him. Ask Him to let you clearly see who He is and to feel His love for you. Ask God to help you understand how to let Him fight your battles and to trust that He can overcome FOR you. Write out your prayer to Him below. Cry out to God to rescue you from any captivity and to truly allow him to deliver you to all the goodness He has promised.

Day 2
YOUR FEELINGS

A GOOD POINT

Feelings are not necessarily facts.

-Unknown

Many, many moons ago, a coworker and friend got fired at the company I was working at. There was a lot of drama going on at the time and all of us who worked in her area were outraged. She didn't deserve it. She was, in fact, a hard worker and did a great job. But, one of the higher-ups didn't like her. That day, with emotions running high, as she packed up her desk, we all vowed we would quit! We would MAKE them take her back or we'd ALL be gone!

Someone once said, *"Emotions make great friends but lousy leaders."* So true.

Emotions make great friends but lousy leaders.

When we had a chance to think about things, we realized that likely nothing would change if we quit. In fact, they probably would have been happy. We'd have nothing (not even unemployment) and they'd get rid of staff who were upset with management. None of us quit.

How many of us as teenagers felt totally justified thinking our parents *"just don't want me to have any fun!"* Yet, for those of us who are now parents ourselves, we realize they were just trying to keep us safe. How many of us have been totally gaga over someone, would have done anything to keep him or her in our lives (and maybe did), only to realize later what a nightmare that would have been? Maybe you are living with some consequences of letting your feelings be the boss of you.

Talk to Jesus about times when trusting your feelings didn't go so well for you.

Some people are more prone to this than others. If you've ever done one of those personality tests you'll either rate as someone who goes more off of *feelings* or those who put *facts* first. Being someone who trusts their feelings isn't always a bad thing. "Feeling" people tend to be very caring and nurturing. Our emotions are an important part of what makes us human. The problem can come when we equate our feelings with truth: *If I feel it, it must be right.* We have to learn to question our feelings. How we do that is by standing them up against what the Bible says.

Obviously, many of our feelings don't need to be questioned. Of course you're going to feel sad when your pet dies. You'll be hurt when a friend betrays you. You will feel pain when you shut your hand in the car door. You'll be happy when you find a five dollar bill on the ground. When we need to question our feelings is when something is potentially life-changing or when something is bothering us.

What types of things qualify? Feelings around relationships (friendships, dating/marriage, family), feelings around finances/major purchases (houses, cars), feelings about who you are (your position, importance, what you do/don't deserve), feelings about things that could or are controlling you (excessive excitement or stress around drugs, drinking, sex, food, appearance, health, death), and spiritual things (salvation, God, evil).

Going through the categories listed above, what are a few things you are currently having pleasant feelings about.

List anything that feels creepy, overwhelming, or somehow negative in your life. Ask Jesus to help you be as specific as you can.

When I was in deep waters, I kept thinking I was condemned to hell and it felt real so I figured it must be right. **Please hear me on this: You will live out what you feel is real.** If you feel condemned you'll live like you are. I didn't take a single picture for three years when I believed that lie. It felt like nothing else mattered. I wasn't really living. I was merely existing. Oh, I was pretty good at faking it for the people around me. They didn't see what was really going on inside. Unfortunately, we can get very good at faking it.

You will live out what you feel is real.

We have to live by facts and not feelings. Just like the Israelites in yesterday's lesson, I too spent years not believing in who God really was. Years in the wilderness thinking God was NOT good. NOT loving. Well, I thought He was, but just to everyone but me. I got sucked into the "poor me" mentality. *God didn't count on this! I'm the one who doesn't fit. I'm the loop hole, the exception to His promises. I am outside of His plan.*

What got me out of that pit was digging in with God. I was in the wilderness for three years, not 30 — not 40 like the Israelites. I started going to God for the truth. The Bible told me over and over again where I was getting it wrong. Who God really is. How He didn't overlook me. How He planned for me to be with Him. How I qualified — and how it was all because He came and got me and had a way to save me.

I started to replace my feelings with facts and that's when everything began to change. I started taking pictures again. Found joy in everything. Had peace I never dreamed of.

Yep, I'm going to ask.

Based on what you wrote on the last page, what feelings are you living by right now?

If we don't keep tabs on our feelings, we can believe something that will ultimately hurt us, hold us down, or hold us back. Or, like the Israelites it can even lead us astray or away from God. That is a sad, unfortunate, joyless place. A place with no future.

Every problem is a spiritual problem.

So, to avoid hanging out in dark places any longer than necessary we need to grab onto truth. God's truth. That happens when we sit with Jesus and get into the Bible for our answers to what life throws at us. In the coming weeks we'll get into how to do that with specific struggles, but over-achingly, **every struggle gets dealt with the same way — by KNOWING GOD. Every problem is ultimately a spiritual problem.** When we KNOW God deeply, that's when everything starts falling into place — when we find our place in Him.

Sit with Jesus. Talk to God

Below are a just a few of many verses that relate to our feelings. As you sit with Jesus, look them up and read them aloud. Ask Him to let you hear what truths He wants to convey about your personal situation. Write down what you hear Him telling you. On a piece of paper, write out the one that speaks to you loudest and memorize it. Put it with the others you'll be gathering this week.

If our hearts condemn us, we know that God is greater than our hearts, and he knows everything.
1 John 3:20

Joshua 1:9

Proverbs 14:12-13

Proverbs 16:32

Proverbs 28:26

Romans 8:1

2 Timothy 1:7

1 John 3:20

Day 3
YOUR FEAR

A GOOD POINT

Everything you want is on the other side of fear.
-Jack Canfield

A few years ago, I was to interview a woman who had been rescued from human trafficking. She had agreed to tell me about her experience and shed some light on how someone gets lured in and how she eventually got out. We spoke on the phone initially to set up a time to meet. She was very cautious as her captor was still living and working in the community. I didn't quite understand why he hadn't been arrested, but her years of abuse and death threats were raw wounds that could not be touched yet. Those who rescued her were aware of who this person was – that he was a prominent and well-known businessman in his community. He would be someone people knew.

She was living in an undisclosed location and just starting the process of rebuilding her life. As we spoke, even her voice sounded broken. She talked about debilitating physical issues. Though a relatively young woman, her outlook sounded like someone decades older. In the brief time I talked to her I heard how her entire life, her entire being, had been shattered. Even though she had been rescued she was not restored. Not even close.

As she shared bits and pieces of her story, her anxiety grew. Suddenly she stopped. She said she just couldn't do this. Couldn't risk it. She feared every detail she gave might put her in danger of him finding her. Her fear stopped her.

Fear will either slow us down or stop us in our tracks. Make us less effective or keep us from living fully or barely at all. That is why evil uses it. It's highly efficient. It steals our power and our voice.

Take a look at the Good Point at the top of the page. We are going to get into what God has to say on the subject of fear, but what we have to realize is that in order to get to *no*-fear we have to push *through* fear. It is not as impossible as it may sound, and as we discussed last week, if you are to the place where the fear of staying the same is not going to cut it anymore, then you will find you have more courage to face the fear than you may think. As Nelson Mandela said, *"I learned courage was not the absence of fear, but the triumph over it. The brave man is not he who does not feel afraid, but he who conquers that fear."* We don't wait for fear to leave before we face it. We do it scared

I learned that courage was not the absence of fear, but the triumph over it. The brave man is not he who does not feel afraid, but he who conquers that fear.

-Nelson Mandela

— but we don't do it alone. The first step is admitting our fear(s). Please be brave and take your biggest fears to Jesus right now. (Please don't skip this. This is so important to do if you are serious about getting rid of your fears, overcoming them, and leaving them behind for good. Look at Jesus and be honest with Him.)

What are you most afraid of?

Remember our Israelite friends in the desert? They didn't want to face their giants because they thought THEY were the ones going up against them. Read Isaiah 41:9-13.

What does God say NOT to do and why? (V10 & V13)

What 3 things does God say He will do for YOU? (V10)

"I will ________________ you and ____________ you; I will ____________ you with my righteous right hand."

Memorization weapon #2

So do not fear, for I am with you; do not be dismayed, for I am your God. I will strengthen you and help you; I will uphold you with my righteous right hand...For I am the Lord your God who takes hold of your right hand and says to you, Do not fear; I will help you. **Isaiah 41: 9-10,13**

In my hardest time, my biggest fear was, *"All of this stuff [God's promises of goodness, rescue, restoration, and salvation] is for other people. It won't happen for me. I'll never get over this or past this. I'll never feel whole or happy."*

But then, I started to read scriptures like those in Isaiah 41 and I couldn't help but feel like God was talking to me when I read, *"I have chosen you."* In the NLT version the next part reads, *"I will not throw you away."* For some reason I, just a little bit, started to believe that. Maybe He hadn't, wouldn't, throw me away like I thought. If I had given my life to Him, believed that Jesus really did do EVERYTHING that was needed to save me, maybe He WAS here to help me. To make me stronger, to get me back on my feet and hold me up. I memorized those verses.

Do you remember we read about the Armor of God in Week 2? Ephesians 6:17 told us that the Word of God is a weapon. I started wielding some against my fear. When it raised it's ugly head I would fight back. I wasn't going to take it lying down anymore. I recited Isaiah 41:9-10 & 13 in retaliation. Out loud when possible. The more I did that, the more I believed it.

Look at those verses again in the margin. Here's something cool I realized.

Which hand does God say He's holding you with?

Which hand of yours does He take?

If Jesus is reaching out with His right hand to take your right hand, what is the most natural way for that to happen? Answer: If you are facing Him. Probably the best posture to have when we feel scared: **Look at Him, not at**

the fear. Right now, reach out your right hand toward Jesus and let Him take hold of you. While you can't see His hand taking hold, God says it's a reality.

I have a wooden box that reads, *"Home is where your mom is."* This is incredibly true for me as my mom is in heaven. Inside the box is an arsenal. Not knives, swords, or those cool metal stars that ninjas use. They are far more dangerous and as it turns out, lethal to fear and evil.

On dozens of scraps of paper are Bible verses and scripture-based thoughts and ideas that I wrote during my hardest time. Some are beautifully written. Others are scrawled on whatever scrap of paper was handy. Perhaps those are the dearest as they represent God giving me a message in a hard moment. Basically, they are notes to remind me who God is. Who I am. Who I should be. As I was writing today's lesson I got them out. I haven't looked at them in years. Most of them I know by heart. Most of them I haven't needed in a long time. They have already done their job and defeated my enemies of fear. One small, blue sticky note made me laugh. It reads, **"You have given up your right to freak out. Trust God!"**

As believers in Jesus, we really have given up our right to freak out. But how do we do that when scary things are not an illusion but a reality? What if our cancer is still there, our PTSD still lurks, our anxiety is off the charts, our addiction still calls to us, and our attacker is at large? We stay close to The One who is going to defeat them.

Here's another one of my weapons. Read Psalm 91 on the right.

Many scholars believe it was penned by Moses and included into the Psalms by David – two huge patriarchs of the faith. This Psalm contains the master plan of how to conquer fear. We just need to understand how to own it and live by it. Ask Jesus to help you understand that this was written for YOU.

If you are following Jesus you have all the rights you need to be the "Whoever" mentioned in verse one. So, imagine yourself in God's Kingdom – where He lives. Pretty impressive? See yourself standing in the shadow of God. Anybody called *The Almighty* must be big – pretty awe-inspiring to be near.

Tell Jesus how you feel about that title for God.

Psalm 91

1 Whoever dwells in the shelter of the
Most High will rest in the shadow of
the Almighty. 2 I will say of the LORD,
"He is my refuge and my fortress,
my God, in whom I trust." 3 Surely he
will save you from the fowler's snare
and from the deadly pestilence. 4 He
will cover you with his feathers, and
under his wings you will find refuge;
his faithfulness will be your shield
and rampart. 5 You will not fear the
terror of night, nor the arrow that
flies by day, 6 nor the pestilence that
stalks in the darkness, nor the plague
that destroys at midday. 7 A thousand
may fall at your side, ten thousand at
your right hand, but it will not come
near you. 8 You will only observe with
your eyes and see the punishment of
the wicked. 9 If you say, "The LORD is
my refuge," and you make the Most
High your dwelling, 10 no harm will
overtake you, no disaster will come
near your tent. 11 For he will command
his angels concerning you to guard
you in all your ways; 12 they will lift
you up in their hands, so that you will
not strike your foot against a stone.
13 You will tread on the lion and the
cobra; you will trample the great lion
and the serpent. 14 "Because he loves
me," says the LORD, "I will rescue him; I
will protect him, for he acknowledges
my name. 15 He will call on me, and I
will answer him; I will be with him in
trouble, I will deliver him and honor
him. 16 With long life I will satisfy him
and show him my salvation."

My Psalm 91

1 Whoever dwells in the shelter of the
Most High will rest in the shadow of
the Almighty. 2 I will say of the LORD,
"He is my refuge and my fortress, my
God, in whom I trust." 3 Surely he will
save [me] from [_______________ or
_______________ or _______________]....
4 He will cover [me] with his feathers,
and under his wings [I] will find
refuge; his faithfulness will be
[my] shield and rampart. 5 [I] will
not fear [_______________ or
_______________ or _______________], the
terror of night, ... 9 If [I] say, "The LORD
is my refuge," and [I] make the Most
High [my] dwelling, 10 no harm will
overtake [me], no disaster will come
near [my] tent. 11 For he will command
his angels concerning [me] to guard
[me] in all [my] ways;...14 "Because
[__________] loves me," says the LORD,
"I will rescue [her/him]; I will protect
[you], for [you] acknowledge my
name. 15 [You] will call on me, and I will
answer [you]; I will be with [you] in
trouble, I will deliver [you] and honor
[you]. 16 With long life I will satisfy
[you] and show [you] my salvation."

Since we qualify as one being addressed in this Psalm, then let's personalize it the rest of the way. On the left, I've changed the references from "you" to "me" or "I" so that it reads more personally. Now finish making this your declaration by filling in the blanks.

> **In verse 3**, the writer lists what God will save him from. Since this is your Psalm, in the first blanks write what you need God to save you from. What was your fear(s) you listed earlier? You can list more than one if you need to.
>
> **In verse 5**, our writer states what he doesn't need to fear now that God is handling them. Like him, write what fears you can let go of.
>
> In the last blank in verse 14, write your name.

Now, go back and read your Psalm.

You may have noticed that there was a stipulation. Something that YOU have to do in order to realize these blessings. Did you catch what it was? Verse 1 touches on it, but look at verse 9 and fill in the blanks. *If I __________, "The Lord is my refuge," and I make the Most High my __________ ...*

In other words: ***When I say I've come to God for help you know I'm serious because I've moved in.*** God will rescue us when we are WITH Him. Not just SAYING we are with Him, but really, truly LIVING with Him. You have to move in with God, and stay there.

What that means is getting ourselves into the mindset that we are ALWAYS with God. We need to start seeing things from a place where He is with us — where He is in charge. Our answers, salvation, and protection aren't out in the world, they are with God. In the coming weeks, we'll learn how to move from fear to power, from living where we are to dwelling with God. For now, realize that the first step to battling fear is believing God's word and using it as a weapon.

Sit with Jesus. Talk to God

Ask Jesus to help you believe that you don't need to be afraid. Start your own arsenal to battle your fears. Write down Isaiah 41:9-10 & 13 and memorize it. When fear comes, read your Psalm 91. Hold onto Jesus and use your weapons EVERY time fear creeps in and start moving to the other side of fear.

Day 4
YOUR WORRY

A GOOD POINT

Your most persistent choice will be to trust [Jesus] or to worry.
-Sarah Young, *Jesus Calling*

I once heard a Bible teacher who was speaking about worry say that she asked God when people would ever stop worrying. What she heard Him say was, ***"They won't stop worrying until they think they don't need to."*** I think that is right.

When I was so scared, and therefore so worried about my situation and whether it would ever be better, I let the concerns churn and churn in my mind. I realized that worry comes down to unanswered questions. I worried because I didn't know if I was right about my situation. I had to know the answers. Worry was how I processed my thoughts in an attempt for answers. That sounds admirable, right? It's not.

I know a woman who worries terribly about her young adult children. For some reason, whenever they travel, driving from one state to another in the course of everyday life, she nearly makes herself sick with worry. Worry that they will crash — that they will die. She always asks for prayers for them during those travels. I don't think her children are unusually inept at driving, or that they have a history of accidents, or even that one of them had a close call once. It's just something that could happen.

You may think that for her situation, there really isn't a question to be answered — at least not one that would likely satisfy her. Her kids could take some specialized courses in driver's training, maybe learn Secret Service security maneuvers, and prove they are prepared, educated drivers. This may help lower her anxiety but the question would still loom. Would there still be a chance her kids could get in an accident? Yes. So, she'd likely still worry.

But, that's not really the question is it? There are deeper questions. Perhaps one is, *"How would I survive if my child dies?"* Because I know this woman to be a Christian, the question really has to be, *"Can I trust God?"*

Every worry we have reveals an area where we don't trust God.

The reality is, if we say we are Christ-followers and have given our lives to Him, every worry we have reveals an area where we don't trust God.
Are you a worrier? Some people are gold-medalists in worrying. Others of

us are more optimistic, but we are all prone to worry now and again. Are you sitting with Jesus? Say hi and settle in with Him. Now, hear Him ask you this question and tell Him your answer.

What are you worried about and why don't you think you can trust Me with it?

Memorization weapon #3

Don't worry about anything; instead, pray about everything. Tell God what you need, and thank him for all he has done. Then you will experience God's peace, which exceeds anything we can understand. His peace will guard your hearts and minds as you live in Christ Jesus.
Philippians 4:6-7 NLT

If your answer had something to do with what you discussed with Jesus in yesterday's lesson on fear I'm not surprised. My worry was directly connected to my fear. Worry and fear are very similar and in some instances would be synonymous – or interchangeable terms. God says the same thing about both. DON'T. Don't worry. Don't be afraid.

In a letter to the believers in the Greek city of Philippi, the Apostle Paul tells them they don't need to worry and what to do instead. Read his instructions in the margin then answer the following questions.

What were they not to worry about?
What were they to pray about?
What were they to tell God?
What should you thank Him for?
After you do those things what will you experience?

Just like I fought against my fear using Scripture, I did the same with worry. I memorized this passage as soon as I found it. It became my mantra. After I recited it I'd do it. *"Father, I'm worried again. I'm not having peace because I'm thinking ___________. Last time I was worried about this in a different way and you showed me that scripture about ______________ and that helped me so much. Thank you for that peace. I'm counting on You to do it again with my new thought. What would I do without You?"*

If I'm honest, I didn't do it that way for a LONG time. Initially, I would just say the verse as if it were like a magic incantation. *Abra-cadabra, bibbity-bobbity-boo, say the verse, God loves you!* It doesn't have a lot of power that way. Scripture is only going to help us when we believe it – when we obey it and behave like it's true. It's like reading the owner's manual for your car. If you don't do what it says after you read it, it's not going to take you anywhere.

The method I listed above, the way the Scripture lays it out, is so great because **1)** You define the problem, **2)** You recall past times when God has delivered – which you will feel very grateful for, **3)** You realize progress is being made in your journey, and **4)** You start to realize that peace IS the payoff.

One more thing you need to know about Scripture is that it's not just words. Read Hebrews 4:12 in the margin on the next page.

What do you think that passage is trying to say?

In the first sentence, what two things does it say Scripture (God's word) is?

When you read things in the Bible, certain passages are going to grab you now and again. They might speak to you, bother you, confuse you, make you cry or smile. **The words are alive and they are going to powerfully change your life.** Again, memorizing and reciting Scripture are good, but it has to be more than that. It's the leaning in with Jesus and listening to what He's trying to get you to understand. You have to spend some time thinking about those words. It's got to get into your bones. You need to let it dig in and dig up what's going on inside you. It's times when you feel exposed by its words that you CANNOT pull back or shut down. That's when you have to look at God and deal with whatever it is. He's there. Not with condemnation but with love, answers, and hope...and peace.

The real win is when you don't even bother to worry when something potentially troubling pops up anymore because you know God's got this. You just go straight to the talking-to-Him-about-it phase. Want to know what my new mantra is? It's not a Bible verse per se, but it's Biblical:

"God KNOWS what's going on."

For my situation, while my initial worry seemed to be one thing, it turned out to be a multi-layered issue. One question answered seemed to quickly lead to another, and another, and another. It took me so long to realize that I could choose to trust God first, instead of defaulting to worrying first. To keep my peace while I waited on His answer. But just like the Bible teacher said, I didn't know then that I didn't need to worry.

I want you to realize something. Go back and circle the first word in the Philippians Scripture on the left. When God talks to us about fear and worry He doesn't say, *"Try not to."* He clearly commands us NOT to. This is not up for debate or thinking, *That's just how I am.* He tells us that because His best for us does not include worry. It does not reflect well on Him. To worry is to cast doubt, to yourself and others, about God's goodness. Worry is simply an indication that you have work to do with God.

Sit with Jesus. Talk to God

If worry is a hot topic for you, keep the discussion going with Jesus now. Write Philippians 4:6-7 to add to your arsenal and memorize it. When worry comes, remind yourself of the steps and get with Jesus about it EVERY time worry appears. Lean in and listen. Watch your worry disappear as trust grows.

For the word of God is alive and powerful. It is sharper than the sharpest two-edged sword, cutting between soul and spirit, between joint and marrow. It exposes our innermost thoughts and desires.
Hebrews 4:12 NLT

Day 5
YOUR THOUGHTS

A GOOD POINT

The thing we look at is the thing we see.
-Hannah W. Smith

"You can think about red. You can think about pink. You can think up a horse. Oh, the THINKS you can think!" says the oh, so wise Dr. Seuss. What we can think of can amuse us, inspire us, entertain us, move us, hurt us, stop us, or downright destroy us.

Do you have THINKS that are not serving you well? This is a good day to make sure you're not alone. Where is Jesus? Is He sitting with you already? Invite Him to scoot a little closer. If that sounded ominous, I don't mean it to be. In fact, I want Him close to you so you feel strong. We are taking charge of some things that have gotten way too much control over our lives.

A Christian woman who is very dear to me, who has spoken such words of life to me straight from the Holy Spirit, shared an experience she had many years before when she was neck deep in her own struggles. (FYI: No one would want to experience even half of what she's gone through.) When she was in a weird place, questioning everything and feeling so confused, sure that no Christian had ever had such odd difficulties like hers, she needed someone to talk to. She had heard about a lady who was known as being a deeply spiritual Christian. She contacted the woman who agreed to meet with her. My friend spent the afternoon pouring out her troubles. She explained what happened.

> She listened patiently enough, and didn't interrupt me, but when I had finished my story, and had paused, expecting sympathy and consideration, she simply said, "Yes, all you say may be very true, but then, in spite of it all, there is God."

In spite of it all, there is God.

My friend pleaded her case further, sure that the woman simply didn't understand the uniqueness and breadth of her situation. The woman assured her she did and reaffirmed her statement, *"In spite of it all, there is God."*

In my friend's journey with God, as well as in my own, we have come to understand that when you know that statement of faith to be true, you will have the right kind of THINKS. As we both also know, getting to those THINKS can be a difficult process. That is, until we get US out of the way.

If you are human, the likelihood is that your thought life is pretty much focused on you. If you are struggling with something, that is probably increased 10X. Nope, not scientific whatsoever, just speaking from experience. The bad news is that if those thoughts are negative, you are destroying your mind. That *is* scientific. Here's the good news, also scientific: You have the ability to change your thoughts.

That might sound like a no-brainer, but if you are feeling bombarded by negative thoughts, struggle with PTSD, depression, anxiety, or have an overwhelming stressor on your plate right now it can feel like you *don't* have control. You do. Let's test it out.

What is your best memory ever?

What is the most beautiful thing you've ever seen?

What natural setting (mountains, beach, waterfall, field, etc.) would you most enjoy gazing at?

When did you laugh the hardest in your life?

Smile. You just controlled your thoughts in a good direction.

So, how do we stop the bad ones? Just like fear and worry, God's got help for us including some verses to put into our arsenal. Let's take this step by step.

Step 1 . Identify and purge negative self-talk

There's a term that seems to be popular right now called "self-limiting beliefs." In other words, things that we have taken on as truth that really aren't. For example, thinking things like *I'll never be able to lose the weight; I've never been good at math; I'll never kick this addiction*, or *That's just how I am,* are all thoughts that can hold you back.

Tell Jesus any self-limiting beliefs that come to mind.

Now, figure out how to re-frame those thoughts so they no longer limit you. For example, *"I've never done this before, but I'm really excited to see if this works so I know if I keep at it – and hang with Jesus – we'll figure it out."*

What's your new spin on your old thought?

Step 2 . Just say NO!

For some of us, there are things that are so dark, so damning, so risky that we cannot allow them ANY space in our brains. EVER! I don't have to detail them if this is an issue for you. You know full well what I'm talking about. Counselors will tell you to reject them immediately by saying, "STOP!" or "NO!" Make your mind up that you will NOT go there. Make your order stern and out loud if possible.

The Bible tells us to take our thoughts captive. Read 2 Corinthians 10:5.

What were the "arguments" and "pretensions" (opinions) against?

What are we to make the arguments and pretensions obedient to?

That might sound a little complicated, but if the Apostle Paul who wrote that were sitting with you right now I think what he'd say is, "*There's going to be a bunch of stuff that tries to sound like a better idea than God — that could draw you away from knowing God. When that stuff shows up, take it to Jesus and tell it who's boss.*"

Dismiss bad thoughts from your mind with a firm "NO!" and give a little shout out to Jesus that He'll need to deal with them. Do it EVERY time — because they will try again and again. Don't forget who is in charge!

Step 3 . Focus on the good stuff

Especially when you're feeling pummeled by negative or scary thoughts, once you've ordered them to stop, you'll need to switch gears and start thinking about something positive. Look at Philippians 4:8 in the margin. Underline each positive thing it lists to think about.

Now, write down some things that qualify. Things you can think of when you need good thoughts.

Memorization weapon #4

Finally, brothers and sisters, whatever is true, whatever is noble, whatever is right, whatever is pure, whatever is lovely, whatever is admirable — if anything is excellent or praiseworthy — think about such things.
Philippians 4:8

Just trying to think of things that are noble and admirable can get your mind off the negative, even if you aren't coming up with something. When I was first introduced to this verse, and battling against destructive thoughts, I'd think of things like new-fallen snow (pure), or a great friend I could always count on (lovely), people who stood up for those who couldn't defend themselves (noble), a couple I knew who always volunteered at disaster sites (admirable). Later I realized that Jesus was all of those things and realistically, if I just started talking to Him I'd be good. Even if it's just random stuff like reciting this Bible verse to Him (or any I had memorized), listing all my favorite things that He ever created (like oranges and trees) or rattling off every good thing Jesus had done for me or others — like all His miracles in the Bible — it works.

Step 4 . Eliminate the bad stuff

What are things that trigger the negative thoughts? Take inventory and eliminate what needs to go. You might have to make some tough decisions. Sit with Jesus and talk it out. Friends might have to go. Facebook might have to go. You may need to switch from a smart phone to a dumb phone. You may need to move. With Jesus you WILL be able to figure it out.

Next, what's not serving you in a way that's positive? What are you feeding your brain? Stop watching so much news, R-rated movies, and joining in with course jokes at work. Ephesians 5:4 in the NLT version says, *"Obscene stories, foolish talk, and coarse jokes—these are not for you. Instead, let there be thankfulness to God."* Pay attention to what doesn't feel right. The Holy Spirit is needling you about some stuff. Don't ignore Him.

Step 5 . Add good stuff

As you're eliminating some bad, you'll have room for something new. I initially rolled my eyes years ago when a friend suggested listening to Christian radio. Yet, once I started tuning in I never went back. If you don't have a church, find one. Ask Jesus to help you find the right one. He will. Join a Bible study, small group, or volunteer. Read Christian books, find Christian friends, watch Christian programs.

Step 6 . Look outward

One big thing we need to realize is that as long as we focus on ourselves, our problems and our issues, that's all we'll see. Go back and read today's Good Point. We will grow our problems if THEY are what we look at most. In Matthew 22:37-40 Jesus laid out what we are to focus on, *"'Love the Lord your God with all your heart and with all your soul and with all your mind.' This is the first and greatest commandment. And the second is like it: 'Love your neighbor as yourself.' All the Law and the Prophets hang on these two commandments."* Did you notice YOU, did not make the list?

Who did Jesus say to focus on (who to love)?

_____________ and ____________________

Think about how to please God. Volunteer, show up, lend an ear. Ask Jesus what you need to do to live out that Great Commandment of loving God with everything you have and loving others well. Focus on doing those two things and you will absolutely find your thoughts going in the right direction.

Step 7 . Always be with Jesus

To have clear and properly focused thoughts we need to stop thinking about ourselves. Completely. If we truly believe the Bible when it tells us that we are ALWAYS with Jesus, then our thoughts simply need to be, *"In spite of it all, there is God."*

Don't forget to put today's scriptures in your arsenal.

Do the wrap up at the end of your week — perhaps on your Day 6. It's a good way to recap what you've learned all week and capture the things that were most important to you.

The Stuff In Your Way

WEEKLY WRAP UP

Write what point, quote, or Scripture stood out most to you this week

This week's memorization verse(s)

I gave you several options this week suggesting you do four. If that's too much, go back and pick the one that is most important to your situation right now.

Hey! I trust you're still hanging in there! This week we started learning to take control of our thoughts and emotions. Particularly the ones that trip us up. One thing I want to clarify is that while we need to take charge of our thoughts and emotions, that does not mean we push things down and pretend like they aren't a problem if they are. If you have, or have had, some trauma in your life that you have NOT gotten peace from God about, you need to do that.

While I know that God can and will heal those deep wounds in your life, no matter what they are, I also know that it can feel overwhelming while you're figuring out how to let Him do that. If you are desperate for help, call your pastor, a trusted friend or family member, or seek professional help. In my hardest season I did that. I did ALL of that. God will work through those people as well.

Interestingly, while some of the time those people were helpful and gave me nuggets of wisdom, Biblical truths, a book to read, and encouragement, many times they did not give me what I hoped for. Sometimes I came away with nothing. But, I think the effort to do those things gave me hope in the most difficult times. In the end, I realized that everything I needed was delivered by God...at the exact right time in order to benefit me, not just in that moment, but FOREVER.

When I went to others, I had to share what was going on and I didn't always give the whole story. I was ashamed. I didn't know how to explain it so they would understand. I worried about what they thought. I know for some of you, if you share what's going on with professionals you could lose your job, your reputation, and more. When I started telling God everything, I realized it wasn't embarrassing. He knew it all anyhow. It was comforting. It felt safe. He truly is the best counselor, comforter, advisor, and fixer.

Too often we believe a doctor, counselor, influential person or even a book or resource is going to fix our problem. They *can* help us, but only Our Creator can truly perfect us. Think of those as tools in His workshop. Weilded in the hand of The Master things can happen, but remember, the most skilled craftsman won't create a masterpiece with just one tool. Don't rely on the tool, rely on The Master.

I know we got into some deep stuff this week that hopefully made you think and provided some insight. In coming weeks, we'll get more into how to continue the battle against these things in our way. In the meantime, you know that old saying, *"If you're going through hell, keep going!"* We will overcome our obstacles and make it through to the glory that awaits on the other side if we just stay on the path with Jesus.

Taking stock: Answer the questions below to process this week's study.

What were some key things that you felt Jesus nudging you about this week?

What was the most positive thing you felt Jesus wanted you to hear this week?

Sit with Jesus. Talk to God

Review the week. For some, there might be a lot to get into but don't get overwhelmed. Start with the most pressing item with Jesus. Tell Him what you're feeling and what you learned. Talk through what your fears are going in and what you're hopeful for. Tell Him what's in your way.

Knowing Jesus Tip: Memorizing Scripture is truly how you weaponize yourself against the enemies of fear, worry, doubt, and evil. I like writing them on index cards. I try to memorize one each week and I take it with me everywhere: Read it at stoplights, when you're brushing your teeth, or waiting in line. In following weeks, I make sure to run through my past verses now and again to keep them stapled to the walls of my mind.

WEEK 4

THE REAL JESUS

Some people think Jesus is a nice guy who loves everyone no matter what they do or how they act. Other people think He's a guy who tried to change the world but ended up getting killed for it. Many people think he died to save us from hell and we'll meet Him when we go to heaven. Who's right and who's creating their own God?

As those who believe Jesus is the Son of God, sent to pay the penalty of our sins with His life, who died and was resurrected three days later, hung out for 40 days after to make sure everybody knew it was true, then went to heaven to get our place ready for us, He sounds like a pretty interesting character. The good news is that right before He left for heaven he said He would be with us always. He'd send His Spirit to live in us so we'd always have Him in our lives. Maybe it's time to get to know who this One is that is taking care of us.

This week we are going to go with Jesus and let Him fill us in on who He really is. We'll have some fun, go to a field full of sheep, see where He lives, and travel somewhere both beautiful and heartbreaking that you've been to before but probably haven't quite experienced like this. Prepare to meet the real Jesus.

Photo: Ian Rinefort . Unsplash.com

Day 1
JESUS OUR GOD

A GOOD POINT

Prayer is putting oneself in the hands of God.
-Mother Teresa

As I was thinking about how God is viewed as one God yet manifesting in three ways: Father, Son, and Holy Spirit — and how to explain that, in any way that doesn't make your eyebrows and your nose try to touch, I thought I'd get some help. I Googled "3-in-1" just to see what popped up. There is 3-in-1 oil, car seats for the wee ones, and printers that can print, scan, and fax (is that even something people do anymore?). The most popular 3-in-1 combo is shampoo/conditioner/body wash. Farther down on the list are mowers that can trim, edge, and cut your grass. We like things that give us more. Somehow, God didn't make the list, even though He started the trend.

The reason I bring up the "God is 3-in-1" concept is because some people can feel really confused by it — and a lot of that happens when people get into deep theological discussion on the depths of "the Trinity" and all that. God is complex and beyond anything we can ever figure out (Isaiah 55:8-9), but how He relates to us from heaven through the Bible, His Son, and His Spirit works really well. We will not need a seminary degree to understand what God wants or how to do life with Him.

Perhaps the biggest question we have is this:

Q: Is Jesus really God?

It's time to give Jesus a seat next to you if you haven't yet. Ask Him to open your eyes, ears, and mind to what we're going to hear from Him today.

R: (Research) To answer this question, let's start by refreshing our minds with a couple of scriptures we looked at back on Week 1, Day 3. Colossians 1:15 says, *"The Son is the image of the invisible God..."* and John 1:1 tells us, *"In the beginning was the Word [Jesus], and the Word was with God, and the Word was God."*

Let's grab a couple more. Look up John 14: 1-11 and fill in the blanks with Jesus' words.

Anyone who has seen _______ has seen ______ ___________. (v. 9)

Read John 10:27-30 and complete the verse below.

I and the __________ are _______. (v. 30)

A: Yes, Jesus is God.
Believe me, if you are still struggling to own that, I completely understand. I grew up in a church that never made the connection that Jesus is God. I thought they were totally separate: God the Father vs. God the Son. The Holy Spirit was hardly even mentioned. So, when I first started really hanging out with Jesus, talking to Him all the time, I kind of felt like I was cheating on God!

I will tell you what helped me, but let's throw in one more question that is related first.

Q: One question people often have is, *"Who do I pray to? Do I pray to God who is my Father, to Jesus who saved me, or the Holy Spirit who lives in me?"*

R: Look at Matthew 6:9-13 in the margin. If you have been in church for any length of time you have likely heard it. You'll hear the answer as soon as Jesus starts the prayer.

The Lord's Prayer

This, then, is how you should pray, "Our Father in heaven, hallowed be your name, your kingdom come, your will be done, on earth as it is in heaven. Give us today our daily bread. And forgive us our debts, as we also have forgiven our debtors. And lead us not into temptation, but deliver us from the evil one."
Matthew 6:9-13

In the Answer blank, write who Jesus tells us to pray to by his example?

A: ____________________
I think it's meaningful that He doesn't say to pray to "my" Father, but "our" Father. He's lumping Himself in with us. When I'm praying I'm usually sitting with Jesus, Him and me together, and we're sitting and praying to *our* Father.

Just a side note, if you are wondering about the Holy Spirit, look up Jude 1:20-21 and fill in the blanks.

But you, dear friends, by building yourselves up in your most holy faith and praying ____ the Holy Spirit, keep yourselves in God's love as you wait for the mercy of our Lord Jesus Christ to bring you to eternal life.

It doesn't say to pray TO the Holy Spirit but IN the Holy Spirit. That means you let your spirit mesh with God's Spirit — be one with God on the inside.

Here's how I got my head around the whole 3-in-1 idea that helps me relate to "Jesus is God" so much better. One scholar put it this way:

*God the Father helps us **eternally**, God the Son helps us **externally**, and God the Spirit helps us **internally**.*

Here's how I would say it: There is just ONE God who created me and wanted me to be with Him forever, who climbed into a human body to come and show me how to live and how to love like He does, and then climbed inside me to make sure I'd get home.

There is just ONE God who created me and wanted me to be with Him forever, who climbed into a human body to come and show me how to live and how to love like He does, and then climbed inside me to make sure I'd get home.

Whether He is God the Father, Son, or Holy Spirit He is 100% God. When we are with Jesus we *are* in the presence of God.

We need to pray to God and we need to get to know Jesus because it's likely we are going to be here for awhile yet. I find a great number of people think that all Jesus came for was to save us from our sins and make us right with God so when we die we can go to heaven. That *is* very important, but New Testament scholar N.T. Wright reminds us that, *"The gospel is really about heaven coming to earth."* Here's how he sees it:

> Imagine a wonderfully gifted musician who was on the verge of playing concertos at the highest level, but who suddenly got caught in a crime for which he'll serve many years in jail. And then suddenly, word comes of a general amnesty. What will he think? He won't just think, "Oh, I don't have to go to jail." He'll think, "At last, I'll be able to play the music like I've never played it before."

Jesus has something for us here, now. We have "music" to play. Look up the following verses and write down some of the things He's got planned.

Matthew 28:19	Make ____________
2 Corinthians 5:20	Be Christ's ____________
Ephesians 2:10	To do ________ ________
Philippians 2:13	Fulfill ______ ________ ________
1 Peter 4:10	Use whatever ________...to ______ others

Before someone has the wrong thought that all God wants us for is to go to work for Him, that's not it at all. Well it is in the sense that a loving parent who has a loving child want to be together. How great is it to spend your day working (in the family business) with the one you love the most?! When you get to know Jesus well, you will feel blessed to be able to serve Him, to be with Him, and what's really great is that you will ENJOY the work! Look at the NLT version of Philippians 2:13 in the margin. We will have the DESIRE to do what pleases God.

For God is working in you, giving you the desire and the power to do what pleases him.
Philippians 2:13 NLT

1 Corinthians 12:5-7 says, *"There are different kinds of gifts, but the same Spirit distributes them. There are different kinds of service, but the same Lord. There are different kinds of working, but in all of them and in everyone it is the same God at work. Now to each one the manifestation of the Spirit is given for the common good."*

In other words, Jesus has something very special in mind just for you that is going to use YOUR gifts, YOUR abilities, and be a blessing in your life for the good of all. (Don't miss that last word — ALL. While you will be blessed in how you serve God, you will never feel totally fulfilled until you are a blessing to others.) What God has planned for you might be hard (it probably will be as most worthwhile things are), but you will know it's what you were built for. Jesus came to guide us to that special purpose, to equip us for it, and to get us engaged as citizens of God's Kingdom.

I've got one more verse for you to look up — Matthew 1:23.

What does Immanuel mean?

God Himself, in Jesus, came down here to be WITH us. He came to save us, to teach us, to lead us, and to engage with us because we are part of His family. We are His beloved child. As we watch Him we'll start to look like Him — bear His image. What does that mean? My kids don't look like me at all. They both take after my husband's family in their physical appearance. Yet, people have remarked on how they "look" like me. It's not their hair or skin color or the shape of their nose. It's how they react to things, mannerisms they've picked up, facial expressions, how we phrase things. People can tell they are mine. Jesus is making sure people can tell we are His. That WE can tell we really, truly, are part of His family and all He is accomplishing.

As I began writing this study, God reminded me that the core of all He does is wrapped up in John 3:16. If you can't recite it by heart look it up and take it in.

God does what He does in our lives because He "SO LOVED THE WORLD." Jesus, God with us, wants to show us His great love starting now...and for all eternity. His Spirit is inside of us, joining with us to guide us all the way.

Sit with Jesus. Talk to God

Have you owned that God loves you. His evidence is shown in His Presence revealed in Jesus who came to save you, guide you, transform you, and to be with you now. Take a few minutes and talk with Jesus about the verses you looked up today and anything that stood out. Discuss how best to pray to your Father, and what plans He has for you.

Day 2
JESUS OUR SHEPHERD

A GOOD POINT

A true shepherd leads the way. He does not merely point the way.
-Leonard Ravenhill

Recently, someone told me about Zhangye Danxia Park in China which is home to the Rainbow Mountains. If you haven't seen them, they appear to be God's paint palette. Truly stunning. Another thing you've probably never seen are herds of domestic sheep roaming free in Erehwon. If you haven't, don't feel too bad because there is no such thing. (Erehwon spelled backwards is Nowhere.) Domesticated sheep would have a very hard time making it on their own. Interesting that we are compared to sheep over and over again in the Bible.

I guess we better see what the attributes of sheep are. Here's what the sheep experts say. **Pros:** Excellent sense of smell, impressive peripheral vision, intelligent, great memories, highly social, and emotionally complex. (And you thought they were just silly sheep.) **Cons:** Considered a prey animal. (Well, that's not good.)

The truth is, while we have a lot going for us, life can seem out to get us. Life — aka Satan, our bad choices, lousy influences, the unexpected, afflictions, other people, us. Wouldn't it be nice to have someone who could watch our backs? Take care of our needs? Protect us? As sheep, I guess we could use a shepherd. [Enter] Jesus.

Let's get some perspective on what Jesus is trying to tell us with this whole sheep/shepherd relationship. As you look up the following verses, remember you are the sheep, He is the shepherd, and answer the questions accordingly.

Read John 10:11-15.

What does a good shepherd do for you? (v. 11)

Check the box if He has. ☐

Read Matthew 9:36. It tells us Jesus felt something for those who *"were harassed and helpless, like a sheep without a shepherd."*

What emotion does Jesus have for us in our difficulties?

Psalm 23

The LORD is my shepherd, I shall not want.

He makes me lie down in green pastures; He leads me beside quiet waters.

He restores my soul; He guides me in the paths of righteousness For His name's sake.

Even though I walk through the valley of the shadow of death, I fear no evil, for You are with me; Your rod and Your staff, they comfort me.

You prepare a table before me in the presence of my enemies; You have anointed my head with oil; My cup overflows.

Surely goodness and lovingkindness will follow me all the days of my life, And I will dwell in the house of the LORD forever.

Psalm 23 NASB

Read Matthew 18:12-14.

If you belong to Jesus and you go astray what's He going to do? (v. 12)

How many is He okay with losing? (v. 14)

Read Luke 15:5-6.

How does He react when He finds His lost sheep?

Jesus sounds like a pretty good shepherd. He's willing to die for us, He's coming after us if we wander away, He has compassion for us, and is not okay with any of us perishing. He rejoices in our found-ness. (Not a word, but I'm going with it.) We have ourselves a pretty sweet deal it seems. If you're not convinced, let's get one more sheep-related scripture. Read Psalm 23 in the margin on the left — even if you know it by heart.

If you have given your life to Christ, say the first part with conviction a few times, stressing each word: THE LORD IS MY SHEPHERD.

Tell Jesus what that means to you — how you live that out.

Now, take the next several minutes and reread Psalm 23. Ask Jesus to help you hear what He is trying to tell you. For example, what do you hear Him telling you about your life when He says, "I shall not want" or "He leads me beside quiet waters?" Review each section and LISTEN to your Shepherd.

Write what you hear Him saying.

Let's walk through some highlights of that scripture. In the beginning sections it conveys that your Shepherd (Jesus) is going to get you comfortable, peaceful. He's going to restore you. Breathe that in for a moment.

Is that a reality for you or a hope?

Next, the writer says there's going to be some dark places, but Jesus has what it takes to keep you safe so you don't have to fear anything.

Do you feel safe with Jesus? Why or why not?

Then, it gets good. Jesus wants you to feel special — like an honored guest at a banquet. He wants you to know you are blessed.

Do you feel blessed by the Shepherd? Share the details.

Finally, Jesus wants you to feel loved every day you're following Him here and He wants you to be confident that you'll live with Him in eternity.

Do you feel loved? Confident in your days and future?

How are you doing as a sheep in Jesus' flock? Sometimes we have to be in the fold for a bit to understand that we are with a GOOD Shepherd. If you've just recently become part of the flock, stay close to the Shepherd to see first hand how good He is.

For others who've been in the flock for awhile, what kind of a sheep are you? Are you a strong and healthy sheep that has obviously been well cared for? Or are you one that has not realized that you ARE in the care of The Good Shepherd? The signs of that are NOT feeling restored, or safe, or calm, or peaceful, or secure, or confident. You may even feel lost, though you are found.

Tell me this, if you went to a farm and saw sickly, starving sheep, would you think it was their fault? No. We'd think they had a terrible care-giver. A terrible Shepherd. We say, *"The Lord is my shepherd,"* but in reality, we aren't letting Him care for us.

We are sheep. We cannot take care of ourselves in some important ways. We cannot control our environment, we will not always see what is going to attack us, and we have little to no defenses for some pretty bad stuff. But, we have a Shepherd. I believe that all too often, we come into the fold, but we stand at the fence and look out, still focused on all of the dangers, all of our worries, when we didn't have a good shepherd. All we need to do is turn away from that view and start focusing on Jesus and the care He is offering.

We come into the fold, but we stand at the fence and look out, still focused on all of the dangers, all of our worries, when we didn't have a good shepherd.

Our job as sheep is just to trust The Shepherd, to stay close, and follow Him.

When I was going through my hardest time, it was so freeing to realize that I WAS just a sheep. Not responsible for saving myself – for eternity or from the pitfalls of this world. The great thing I discovered about my Shepherd is that when you fall in a pit, even when you forget to call on Him sometimes – forget to reach up to Him, He still shows up to pull you out again and again. That is a good, good Shepherd. (Note: I finally got wise and started staying closer to Him. Funny how there aren't any pits when I follow Him.)

Sit with Jesus. Talk to God

Ask Jesus to give you a visual of where you are in His flock. If you see that you are by the fence or off in the corner, talk to Him about why you are doing that. Ask Jesus to come and pick you up and put you on His shoulders to help you gain a better perspective.

Note: Tomorrow, we're going somewhere special so carve out some private time when you can be alone and uninterrupted.

Day 3

JESUS OUR SAVIOR

A GOOD POINT

The cross shows us the seriousness of our sin —
but it also shows us the immeasurable love of God.
-Billy Graham

When my husband and I hit a milestone wedding anniversary, we celebrated by going to Maui. People who'd been there would suggest sights and tell us how beautiful it was. The Road to Hana was mentioned over and over, but until you stop along the way and feel the spray of the waterfalls and hike up into the adjacent hills to see and touch the smooth wood of the Rainbow Eucalyptus trees, it's just not the same.

One day, we drove to Maui's volcano. Haleakala Crater, whose summit is 10,000+ feet above the Pacific, was described by author Jack London as a place of *"incomparable grandeur."* What I remember most isn't the view from the top, but the ride to the top.

One thing many tourists like to do is bike-ride *down* the road that winds round and round the crater. Not many pedal to the top. There is a bus that will take you up there for a price. I'm not sure if the young couple from Germany we met at the bottom didn't have the money or if they just missed the bus, but they asked us if we'd give them and their bikes a lift to the top. While we had a very small rental car, we figured it was all part of the adventure.

What I remember is chatting with this young couple and being impressed with their sense of adventure — they were basically hoboing it as evidenced by their pungent smell as those who were only "bathing" when they explored the ocean. It did not seem offensive, just part of the story. One aspect of the drive is that you come to a point where you are actually driving through the clouds. Yep, it's pretty great. Better in person than in pictures or stories.

Today, I want to take you somewhere — to experience something for yourself. It's somewhere you've likely been before, but your experience may have been more like looking at pictures — hearing it second-hand. I want you to experience it for yourself. As I mentioned yesterday, this is another one of those times you'll want to have total privacy and uninterrupted focus for awhile. If you need to adjust your schedule for this one do it. We're headed to the cross.

If you're like me, you've probably heard the story of Jesus being crucified and how He rose from the dead. Obviously, we covered it a bit in the first week of our study. Hearing what He did for you is different than going through it with Him. I don't want you to be worried in any way. We are focusing on the beauty and the meaning more than the gruesome details.

Just a quick side note, if you've never seen *The Passion Of The Christ* movie directed by Mel Gibson that came out in 2004, I do think it's something that every believer should watch. It does show the brutality of what Jesus suffered for us and while gut-wrenching to watch, we graphically see the severity of our sin and the sacrifice it took to pay for it. Today, however, we are going to go to the cross with Jesus in a different way.

To get started let's get a little background. Look up Hebrews 9:22 and answer the question below.

Why did Jesus have to shed His blood for us?

Way back in the Old Testament, after God had chosen His people, He laid out the laws that would guide them. (If you are an overachiever you can read about them in Leviticus chapters 1-7.) When you boil it all down, what it says is this: People are going to pay for their many and varied sins by providing a substitution. Another living thing will need to die in their place.

Still hanging out in the Old Testament, Read Isaiah 1:18.

What color do your sins start out as?

What color will they be?

Keep those scriptures in mind as we head out. We'll make some stops along the way to get our bearings now and again. Let this be a slow journey. Let time stop. See yourself in every moment. This is framed by what I experienced when I went to the cross with Jesus, but this needs to be YOUR time.

Think about what's happening, how you're truly feeling. If part of the story doesn't feel authentic for you, tell Jesus why and what YOU are experiencing. Ask Jesus to take you back to that day some 2000 years ago. The day that He made a way for you. The day He paid for all your sins. The day that changed everything for you from here on out. The day on the cross of Calvary.

Are you with Him? Just look at His face. You're not going to see what they've done to his body, you're going to see what's beyond that. He's smiling at you.

All of the preliminary stuff has happened. He's been condemned and He and the man on the road to Golgotha have carried his cross to the place where

He'll be crucified. The soldiers are getting everything ready. Jesus is laying on his back — on the ground — waiting for them to begin. You kneel down in the dirt next to Him. People are around, but you don't hear them. This is too personal. It's just you and Jesus. He has such a peaceful look that just draws you in and keeps you focused on Him.

What do you feel as you gaze at Jesus in this place? Tell Him.

Time seems to stand still. You feel a strange peace and yet you feel like someone is pushing you down. You look at yourself to see what's going on to discover you aren't wearing your normal clothes. Instead, you fit right in with the people of that era. You're wearing a robe — except yours is black. All over it, in deep red letters, are written all your sins. To see them all exposed it feels overwhelming. Can there really be so many?

Some you recognize and know all too well. Others are ones you'd nearly forgotten about. Many are ones that were so day-to-day you stopped thinking about them as sins. Some of them are written small, many are large and bold.

What are you reading spelled out on your robe?

You know that Jesus has seen them all too. Not just read them but SAW them as they happened.

What do you feel as you realize He has seen ALL of your sins?

It would be understandable if a great shame welled up in you. If your face burned in embarrassment. For others who have been here, though those feelings of guilt seem appropriate, they feel okay with Jesus seeing them. It doesn't feel strange or condemning for some reason. Perhaps they knew what was coming.

Regardless of how you feel, the realization that He is going to suffer for YOU — DIE for you — BECAUSE of you — is a lot to swallow. You know it's almost time. The soldier has the nails and the hammer ready.

As you look at Jesus, what are you thinking?

Jesus just continues to look at you with nothing but complete devotion and love. Some have wondered, *Why isn't He worried! Why doesn't He stop this!* or *Isn't there another way?!* Others have thought, *I don't matter! Don't waste this on me!*

You feel you should say something.

What do you want to say to Jesus?

Maybe you put words to your thoughts. Maybe in the end it came out something similar to, *Don't do this! You don't have to do this — not for me.*

What do hear Jesus say back to you?

If you know The Shepherd at all, The One who lays down His life for His sheep, then what you should have heard is love. What Jesus says to us all as He gave His life on the cross to save us and pay for our sins is the same. Jesus just smiles and says in all seriousness, *"You are worth it."*

Write down anything you'd like to capture so far.

They have taken Jesus and put him on the cross. Something more is coming. His work is just getting started, so let's get ready to go back. Take one more look at Isaiah 1:18.

Q: What would happen if you dipped your robe, covered with the red letters spelling out all of your sins, into blood?

A: You wouldn't be able to read the sins anymore. They'd be covered.

Now, read Revelation 7:14.

How did they get white robes?

Jesus, the perfect Lamb (the perfect sacrifice), washed our sin-covered robes in His blood and purified them.

When Jesus died, they laid Him in a tomb. Let's head there. Read John 19: 38-42 and 20:1-18.

Mary Magdalene has just experienced Jesus on the other side of the tomb. Now, it's your turn. Head back 2000 years where you left Jesus. They crucified Him and He's been dead since Friday, but dawn is about to break Sunday morning. You have a big advantage from Mary and the disciples — you know what happens: Jesus is going to get back up! See yourself, alone, at the tomb that early Jerusalem morning waiting on Jesus. Look at your robe.

What color is it?

Sit with Jesus. Talk to God

Talk to God about what you experienced today. Discuss how you feel about the color you see your robe now. Did today add to your understanding of what Christ did for you that day? Tell Him if it moved you and if not ask Him why not.

Tomorrow, we'll finish our time in Jerusalem as Jesus exits the Tomb, and see a new concept of His relationship with us.

Day 4
JESUS OUR HOME

A GOOD POINT

The best of it is, God is with us.

-John Wesley

Several years ago, my sister-in-law was planning on coming to visit. We wanted to do something special and decided we should go to the Black Hills in South Dakota as she'd never been there, nor my father-in-law who'd be joining us. If you've never been there, that's where Mount Rushmore is. It's a picturesque area with lots to see and do — and just a few hours away from us.

Because my father-in-law was 80, we wanted to have a home-base that was a little more comfortable than a hotel room. I asked my friend, who had often mentioned their Black Hills cabin, if they ever let friends borrow it and explained our situation. I knew they went there with their kids so assumed it had at least three bedrooms.

After checking what dates we thought we'd need it, she said that would work — if we didn't mind sharing the cabin with her and her daughter who planned to be there that same time. Then she added, *"But you won't even know we're there – we'll be on the other side."* I was slightly baffled but agreed, knowing she and her daughter were delightful and very hospitable.

When we arrived my expectations were blown out of the water. The "cabin" could more accurately be described as a "secluded retreat center" with its 13 bedrooms, 7 bathrooms, and many amenities. It was more than we could have asked or imagined.

In my Father's house are many rooms; if it were not so, I would have told you. I am going there to prepare a place for you.
John 14:2

When people think about dwelling with God, they typically envision heaven. After all, in John 14:2, Jesus says He's going to the Father to prepare a place for us. Not here, but there. I'm guessing that place is going to be more than we could ask or imagine as well. However, most of the references in the Bible about dwelling with God are in the here and now. It doesn't take much thought to wonder why that is: There are far too many dangers here to be out on our own. So, let's get ready to move in with God.

Do you have Jesus with you? If so, go through the following Scriptures with Him, then circle any words that indicate various types of structures that God represents. I've done the first one that appears for you.

2 Samuel 22:2 — *[David] said: The "LORD is my rock, my fortress and my deliverer; my God is my rock, in whom I take refuge; my shield and the horn of my salvation. He is my stronghold, my refuge and my savior....*
Psalm 31:20 — *In the shelter of your presence you hide them from the intrigues of men; in your dwelling you keep them safe from accusing tongues.*
Psalm 91:4 — *He will cover you with his feathers, and under his wings you will find refuge; his faithfulness will be your shield and rampart.*
Proverbs 1:33 — *but whoever listens to me will live in safety and be at ease, without fear of harm.*
Proverbs 18:10 — *The name of the LORD is a fortified tower; the righteous run to it and are safe.*

Now, go back through the verses and, in the margin, write down what you get from dwelling with God. Ask Jesus to help you see all the advantages mentioned. See if you can name at least seven. I started the list for you. *If you have trouble identifying them, look up Psalm 91 (that we studied intently last week, Day 3) for a whole bunch of benefits.*

How do those ideas speak to you? Tell Jesus.

Benefits of living with God:

1. Stability
2. Protection
3.
4.
5.
6.
7.

While ideas of God being a "fortress" or "stronghold" might make us feel secure and sheltered, it doesn't necessarily convey a comfy, cozy place that we'd want to spend all our time. Most of us desire a more comfortable place — a home. God gets that so He throws out the example of sheltering you with His feathers. If you're wondering what kind of a bird he's talking about, look up Matthew 23:37 and fill in the blanks: *"...how often I have longed to gather your children together, as a _____ gathers her ________ under her wings,..."*

God displays Himself as a mother hen — soft, nurturing, loving, protective. Perhaps this is the most accurate depiction of dwelling with Him. He tells us to come to Him and get under His wings. His protection and security doesn't happen in a *place* but WITH Him.

God sent Jesus, *Immanuel* — God with us, to be our home until we get to heaven. The beauty is, we don't have to move locations to be with Jesus, we just have to remember that He moved in with us. Read what Jesus says in John 14:20-21 then write the appropriate names in the illustration below.

God sent Jesus to be our home until we get to heaven.

Yesterday we left off waiting at the tomb for Jesus. It's time to finish up our journey there so let's go back now. You were looking at the color of your robe when we parted yesterday. (If you have accepted Christ's sacrifice on the cross for your sins and believe He conquered death — that He is the Son of God, then your robe is white. Regardless of how you feel about what color *you* think it should be, it is white. God says so.)

Jesus is risen! He's coming out of the tomb. It's just the two of you. If you remember from yesterday's Scripture, when Mary saw Jesus coming out of the tomb, Mary didn't recognize Him at first. Something was different apparently, though it doesn't say what. Ponder this with Jesus as you see Him.

What does He look like compared to how He looked before crucifixion?

I wonder if He's different because He's back to the real, untarnished version before the world beat Him up. Though it couldn't touch His soul, it did its worst physically.

Does this thought resonate with you? How would you be different if your mind and your body were back to an untarnished version?

Based on John 14 saying you are in Christ and Christ is in you, I want to give you a visual that might help you grasp this reality:

As Jesus comes out of the tomb, He smiles at you just a little bit differently than before. He's smiling at someone who is not a victim now, but a victor! He fought the battle for you against death, sin, and evil and won. They do not need to be part of your story anymore. Now, the future awaits and all the plans He has for you.

"Are you ready?" He asks. Since you gave your life to Him you figure that's a rhetorical question. You wait for Him to lead the way. Instead He moves toward you, arms open. As He embraces you it's like a hug, but so much more — like a powerful explosion of light enveloping you, inside and out! As you look down the front of you, at your arms and legs, you see yourself, but He is now part of you, encompassing you in Himself. You are clothed in a glowing, white light. Inside you sense a change. It's warm and peaceful, and happy. You hear Him talking to you — from the inside. This is HOME.

This is how you do life from here on out: IN Him.

How does this idea make you feel?

Being at HOME with God is simply being aware that God is always with you now. It's walking through life in His shadow — in His presence. When I was a rebellious teen, you'd never know it if one of my godly grandmothers was around. I would never say or do anything in their presence that would dishonor or offend them. It's kind of like that with God. When you are aware of Him being with you, you will find the conviction and power to be better. You may think it's pretending to be better when you're really not. What you may be surprised to find is that who you are with God is actually the REAL you.

Who you are with God is actually the real you.

When you are at HOME, focusing on your Father, you will learn to lean on Him when you don't know what to do. It's realizing that God wants to be a part of everything you're doing. Not having any cares or worries because your DADDY is there to help you. You will be HOME each time you realize He is with you and you act like He is.

The biggest problem you will face is STAYING HOME. Just like the sheep who stand at the fence and look out at their old life, nothing changes if we don't change our focus. If we don't keep checking on our whereabouts, we'll find that we've "left home." We go back to thinking we live in our troubled lives alone. Think WE have to deal with it all. Forget we have a HOME and a SAVIOR — that we have a shelter to run into where we are ALWAYS safe, cared for, loved, and protected. If you are sheltering from evil and the enemies that drag you down then it's even more imperative that you don't leave God's shelter!

When I was doubting God and believing all the lies, all the negative stuff that the world tells you, I was worried, scared, and miserable. When I realized that everything IS in God's control, that even the bad things can be used for good (Romans 8:28), I put a stake in the ground that I was absolutely trusting God. That's when the worry and fear left. If I'm being totally transparent, for quite awhile I pulled the stake up nearly every day too — which put me back in fear and feeling "homeless" once again.

Over time, I learned how to stay HOME and trust God with more and more. I was transformed. My life was transformed. Everything I have put in God's care so far (and it's been a truckload!) has come out just fine. Actually, better than fine — it's been more than I could ask or imagine! When I'm at HOME with Jesus, I'm safe and cared for. That's where there are answers. That's where peace and joy are. That's where I see the untarnished version of me.

I pray that out of his glorious riches he may strengthen you with power through his Spirit in your inner being, so that Christ may dwell in your hearts through faith.
Ephesians 3:16-17a

Sit with Jesus. Talk to God

Look up and read (aloud if possible) Ephesians 3:16-21. Ask Jesus to help you see yourself at home in Him. Ask Him how you learn to stay HOME and start sharing your whole life with Him.

Day 5

JESUS OUR EVERYTHING

A GOOD POINT

Jesus does not offer to make bad people good
but to make dead people alive.
-Ravi Zacharias

In the summer of 1859, a daredevil appeared on the scene in New York City. Charles Blondin, in his early 30s, strung a 1,300 foot rope across Niagara Falls with the intention of walking across it. No net, no safety harness. Swarms of spectators gathered and bets were taken as to whether he would fall to his death. He did not. Instead, he not only walked across, but came back, this time carrying a large camera on a stand. He stopped in the middle, set up the camera, threw the black cloth over his head and snapped a photo of the crowd on the American side.

Subsequent crossings ensued with Blondin upping his game each time. He enjoyed a glass of wine (hoisted up from a boat below), ate cake at a table, and even carried a stove, started a fire, and cooked an omelet.

One story is told that at a particular performance he planned to push a wheelbarrow across. With many having heard or seen his previous exploits his manager shouted to the crowd, *"Do you think he can do it?"* A unanimous cry responded, *"Yes!"* The manager upped the ante, *"Well what if we put a man in it? Do you still think he can do it?"* Again, the group agreed as one, *"Yes!"* The manager hawked one last time, *"Do I have a volunteer?"* The crowd fell silent.

Imagine that instead of Blondin pushing the wheelbarrow it is Jesus. We look at all He has done and we believe in His ability — until it gets personal. How do we put our lives, our everything, into Jesus' care?

Where is Jesus right now? See Him standing there with a wheelbarrow.

Tell Him if you feel like you would climb in without hesitation and if you'd let Him take you wherever He wanted to go. Jot your thoughts.

Just to make sure you're considering everything that might come along on this ride, evaluate the following and see if it changes your mind. Put a check in the box if you are still getting in with Him.

I'd get in with Jesus even if...

1. ☐ He takes me away from _______________ or him/her away from me.
   someone important to you
2. ☐ He has a different career/job in mind.
3. ☐ He doesn't let me continue _______________.
   you know what it is
4. ☐ I never get to have _________________ again.
   what comes to mind
5. ☐ my future doesn't include _________________.
   something important to you

Did your thoughts change about getting all in with Jesus? Before we freak ourselves out on all that Jesus MIGHT do in our lives, let's remember the Bible assures us (as believers in Christ) that we NEVER need to be afraid and we NEVER need to worry. If you are experiencing fear or worry right now you are either believing lies or playing out the story wrong.

To get some perspective, let's fill in the blanks with some potential answers and play the thoughts that, if we're honest, could really be going through our minds.

1. Is Jesus going to take me away from my boyfriend? I know why He'd want to – I want to take me away sometimes, but what would I do? I'd be homeless! I don't make enough money! Jesus, you know that can't happen, right?!

2. I worked hard to get this job. I've still got student loans and the house and our cars to pay for. I like being a big deal, people under me. I make a lot of money. My dad is counting on me to make him proud. My family needs me to make this kind of money. Jesus, you understand.

3. Okay, it's obviously my eating "disorder." I know how I'd feel, how I'd look, if I just let this go and it would not be good. I've just got to keep it in check. Yeah, I know I haven't always done that well, but Jesus, we've talked about this forever. I don't want to feel this way, but I just do. We both know it's not going to change.

4. Man, a few things came to mind. I guess sex is the biggie. Come on! A guy can't be expected to give that up! I know the only way You allow that is one way and that isn't how I've been living. I'd go crazy thinking about it all the time so how would that be better?

5. Well, so far this one is true: children. I want to be a mom so badly. We've tried everything the doctors said and all we have is heartbreak, but thinking about no children is even worse. I've been with you Jesus – I really can't fathom why this would be a "no."

To sum up what all of those thoughts come down to would be, *"Jesus, I can only trust you if..."* Or, at the very least, *"I can trust you with everything except..."*

Go back and read the Good Point at the beginning of today's lesson. When we gave our lives to Christ, He saved us from death. Until we are able to die to ourselves we'll never truly live. The thinking that we *can't* change, *couldn't* live without certain things or people, *must* have this job or that experience, could *never* stop doing this or that, keeps us from living — REALLY living.

If we are honest with ourselves, many of us don't actually want to give up total control and rely on Jesus from here on out. Some of us would just like Him to take away the pain, the addiction, the desire, the sickness, the loss, the emptiness, the memories, and return us to how things were before. We would simply be happy with returning to the status quo.

Paul's sufferings:

God says that's not enough — He's in the LIFE business. Good enough is not what He has planned for His kids — because it never is.

Part of the reason we don't trust is because we are great at spinning dire stories. The problem is that once we spin our worst case scenarios we stop the story and leave ourselves there. God's not saying life won't get ugly, but what He does promise is that it's just temporary.

Look up 2 Corinthians 4:17 and write it below.

If ever a Bible verse made people want to slap someone this may be it. I hear you, *"Seriously! 'Light troubles' when my child has leukemia!"* or *"Momentary?! I've been struggling with addiction for 20 years!"*

Paul, who wrote that Scripture, was well acquainted with hard things. Read 2 Corinthians 11:24-27 and in the margin write down all he'd been through.

When he mentions, *"once I was pelted with stones,"* that is saying it lightly. They stoned him until they thought he was dead (Acts 14:19). Paul's been through the wringer following Jesus. So why on Earth would he say that this stuff is just, *"light and momentary troubles?"* He tells us in Philippians. Look up Philippians 3:7-8 and fill in the blanks below.

(v. 8) "I consider ______________ a loss because of the ______________ worth of ______________ Christ Jesus my Lord,"

What did Paul consider worthless (a loss)

On the other side of all that suffering, Paul looked back and saw that knowing Jesus was worth it all. That losing everything was nothing to him because the value of Jesus in his life was of such worth.

Jesus told a couple of parables of what doing life with Him is like.
Read Matthew 13:44-46.

What were the people who found the treasures willing to give for them?

How did the man in the first example feel about it?

Stories are told in the Bible of some individuals that were in the wheelbarrow with God. Daniel decided that he would not waver in his beliefs and honoring God even though he was taken captive to a new land with completely different beliefs. When those around him wanted to get rid of him they used his faith against him, yet he didn't waver. That loyalty got him thrown into the lion's den. God rescued him (Daniel 6).

Three of Daniel's friends did the same and stood by their decision to be all-in with God. When they refused to follow everyone else in worshiping a statue of the king the three were thrown into the fiery furnace. As the king looked on to watch them burn he instead witnessed a miracle.
"Look!" he answered, "I see four men loose, walking in the midst of the fire; and they are not hurt, and the form of the fourth is like the Son of God." -Daniel 3:25 (NKJV)

When you're in the fire, Jesus shows up. Shadrach, Meshach and Abednego came out of the fire unharmed. Maybe the most powerful part of the story is what happened before they were thrown in. As the king threatened them with death they confirmed their stance.
"Shadrach, Meshach and Abednego replied to him, King Nebuchadnezzar, we do not need to defend ourselves before you in this matter. If we are thrown into the blazing furnace, the God we serve is able to deliver us from it, and he will deliver us from Your Majesty's hand. But even if he does not, we want you to know, Your Majesty, that we will not serve your gods or worship the image of gold you have set up." -Daniel 3:16-18

Even if God didn't give them the outcome they hoped, they chose Him.

Jesus is a radical guy — a radical God. He doesn't do things like the world. He doesn't always do what WE want. He does what is right and what is best. When Jesus started telling His disciples that He was going to die and three days later be raised Peter got in His face about it. Look up Matthew 16:21-27.

Who did Jesus say Peter was acting like?

Peter couldn't wrap his head around the fact that winning meant dying.

They expected the Messiah to come in power and take control. As theology professor Randy Harris said, *"They thought they were on a power boat. Turns out it was a death ship."* Jesus doesn't tell you to take up your sword, but to take up your cross. While Jesus came as a servant, He didn't come to serve us. He came to show us how to serve.

Jesus saved us from death by dying. Real life comes on the other side of death. First, accepting Christ's death, then accepting our own. We will only TRULY live when we die to ourselves.

Jesus has to be your everything or nothing will really change.

Jesus has to be your everything or nothing will really change.

Jesus WILL show up for you in ways that you can't even fathom, if you get out of the way and let Him. It very likely won't be in the way you think, how you see it, or based on your life plan. Instead, He will give you a story like nobody else's that you'll look back on and say, *"Man, that was one rough ride! But what Jesus did, what He showed me, and what I came away with is something I wouldn't have missed for anyone or anything! Nothing compares to knowing Jesus!"* I know this to be true, because of what Jesus has done for me — and I've got a ways to go in this journey yet (depending on God's plan).

Go back to the passage in Matthew 16 and reread verse 25 in the margin.

Listen to Jesus and write what you think He's trying to tell you below.

For whoever wants to save their life will lose it, but whoever loses their life for me will find it.
Matthew 16:25

In case you are wondering, someone did trust Blondin enough to go across the falls — on his back. It was his manager, Harry Colcord. Blondin gave these instructions before they embarked on the journey across the perilous:

> "Look up, Harry.... you are no longer Colcord, you are Blondin. Until I clear this place be a part of me, mind, body, and soul. If I sway, sway with me. Do not attempt to do any balancing yourself. If you do we will both go to our death."

Sit with Jesus. Talk to God

Ask Jesus to help you be all-in with Him. To die to yourself, to kill your expectations and plans, and to learn how to be part of Him — mind, body, and soul — so that you can truly LIVE. Take a stand to let Jesus be your everything.

The Real Jesus

WEEKLY WRAP UP

Do the wrap up at the end of your week — perhaps on your Day 6. It's a good way to recap what you've learned all week and capture the things that were most important to you.

Write what point, quote, or Scripture stood out most to you this week

Hey! Are you feeling more connected to Jesus? When we think about giving our entire lives to Jesus and letting him run the show it can feel a little odd. Maybe even scary. Remember, this is not a hostile takeover of your life. It's actually an apprenticeship.

Not too long ago, I felt like I was messing up continually. I was sure I was just this big disappointment to God. I was sitting on the floor telling Him all this and I said, *"God, I give up! Just shove me out of the way and take over!"* In my mind I saw myself letting go of a large steering wheel, like one on a pirate ship, and plopping down on the deck. Not what I'd call *surrendered* but more *defeated*. Of course Jesus was right there. Without missing a beat He pulled me up, set me in front of the wheel again, and said, *"Let me show you how."* Just like a dad teaching his kid to fish, He wrapped his arms around mine to guide me. Yep, this is exactly who Jesus is. Yep, this is the kind of mental goings-on you can look forward to.

When we give our lives over to Jesus we'll still have to do the work. But He will show us how. We'll have to listen and we'll have to DO. No sitting on the sidelines. When we put on the Jesus jersey it's because we're a player not a fan. When we move in with God we're not going to become lazy, irresponsible, couch potatoes but active participants in our Father's work. Participating in our transformation and ultimately in serving Him — which equals serving others.

I just found it curious that my mind saw a pirate ship — not a pleasure cruise. Jesus is way too radical to drive something tame! He'd look at the people on a pirate ship and think, *"I see a lot of potential there."* Jesus is so different isn't He? He makes being the "good guy" seem like the "baddest" role of all. Who doesn't want to be like that?!

When it all comes down to it, when we can get over ourselves and just focus on Jesus we will get to where we want to go. As I've said before, it may not be where you THINK you want to go, but it will absolutely be where you WANT to be. A lot of what we'll need to do to get to that place will not make sense at first. It will likely take you awhile to think like Jesus and stop thinking about

This week's memorization verse

The LORD is my shepherd, I shall not want.

He makes me lie down in green pastures; He leads me beside quiet waters.

He restores my soul; He guides me in the paths of righteousness
For His name's sake.

Even though I walk through the valley of the shadow of death, I fear no evil, for You are with me; Your rod and Your staff, they comfort me.

Psalm 23:1-4 NASB

There are two more verses of this Psalm if you want to tackle the whole thing all the better!

things like the world does. Just keep looking at Him. Let Him guide you in everything and make adjustments to the sails as you go. When you realize all that the REAL Jesus is, you'll know how to be, where to go, and what to do. That's when you'll get to REAL life.

Taking stock: Answer the questions below to process this week's study.

What were some key things that you felt Jesus nudging you about this week?

What was the most positive thing you felt Jesus wanted you to hear this week?

Sit with Jesus

What's standing out from all the different characteristics of Jesus? How does that make a difference in your life and circumstances right now? Tell Him what you're enjoying, what you're struggling with, and what you need help with at this point in the journey.

Knowing Jesus Tip: It's a good idea when looking up scripture to take a look around the verses you're keying in on so you get context. See what's going on by reading a few verses before and after it to be able to answer a few key questions like who's talking, who are they talking to, where are they, and what's going on? A big part of knowing Jesus and what God wants happens when we know what His Word (*The Holy Bible*) says.

WEEK 5

THE HARD ROAD

"*In this life, you will have trouble.*" That's what Jesus said. As I look back, while there were a few bumps in the road my first few decades on the planet, compared to what happened later, my early years were basically a cake walk. Then, in less than a two-year time frame I found myself walking the hardest road of my life — I was personally struggling just to keep my head above water and that's when my niece fatally overdosed, and on the one-year anniversary of her death my mother was killed. Suddenly, I knew "hard" well.

Why do bad things happen? Why does it have to be so hard? As I journeyed down the hard road with God, I realized some things about the so-called "bad" things of life. I realized that when you follow Jesus on that road you get a perspective, an education, and insights that I'm not sure you can get on the smooth road we all want to be on.

This week, we'll travel down some rocky paths and see why God creates or allows some hard roads in our lives. Perhaps you are traveling on one now. If so, pay attention traveler because you are in the perfect place to see and learn things that can be unforgettable and life-changing for your journey. Step onto the hard road with Jesus.

Photo: Johnathan Borba . Unsplash.com

Day 1

PAY ATTENTION

A GOOD POINT

Pain insists upon being attended to. God whispers in our pleasures, speaks to us in our consciences, but shouts in our pains. It is his megaphone to rouse a deaf world.
-C.S. Lewis

Knowing Jesus Tip:
It's a good idea to jot down your thoughts as you sit with Jesus – especially if you can't speak out loud. Sometimes you'll find what flows from your pen is more than what you come up with in your thoughts.

In the studies this week, I'm going to pose some valid reasons as to why bad things happen based on what the Bible says. This is not to imply that all, or even the specific ones we'll cover, are the reason for any hard roads in YOUR life. These are to get you thinking. To sit with Jesus to question and consider the possibilities. It's all about learning and leaning in to find out what the point is for pain, heartbreak, suffering, loss, or other hard seasons. Make sure you start each day with Jesus next to you. Take a minute and settle in with Him. Tell Him what you're feeling as we move into this week's topic.

Several years ago, I heard the president of a Christian humanitarian aid organization tell an incredible story of something that he witnessed when Ethiopia was a communist nation and Christianity was illegal. The church there had moved underground and only met in secret, in the cover of night. Their pastor took risks often, facilitating funerals – of which there were many. This is what I captured as the president shared the story:

> Despite warnings from the local government to stop, a pastor continued to openly share the gospel and pray at funerals. The government officials decided enough was enough and it was time to make an example of him. They arrested Pastor Tadessa and sentenced him to death. They decided on the electric chair. The chair was erected in the center of town where everyone could see. The few members of the humanitarian group could do nothing but watch from a distance. The pastor was marched out and asked if he'd like to say any last words to his God. He did and he prayed. They put him in the chair and flipped the switch. Nothing happened. They took him back to his cell vowing that he would die the following day.
>
> The humanitarian team watched out of sight again the next day. As promised, the pastor was seated in the chair. Once again, they asked the pastor if he had any last words to his God. He prayed. The switch was thrown and an eruption of electricity flowed, but not as expected. Instead, it blew out power throughout the entire area. The pastor was very much alive.

> Furious and frustrated, the officials released the pastor, yelling at him to leave. Once he was a safe distance from town, walking up a dirt road, with smoke still rolling from his hair, we caught up to him.
>
> The team couldn't believe what they had just witnessed! They were marveling at what God had done. Elated they pressed the pastor, "So what do you do after something like that?!"
>
> Pastor Tadessa answered, "I'm going to a funeral."
>
> Nearly speechless, they said, "We'll be praying for you!" The pastor replied, "I'll be praying for your church too." They were a little baffled and asked, "What do you pray for for us?"
>
> He faced them and said, "Though the Ethiopian Church's suffering is severe, it's not nearly the suffering what you in the West are experiencing. Due to the pressure here, the Ethiopian Church prays all day long. I hear that it is possible that Christians in the West might not pray even once a day. Here, we must risk our lives to gather together because we need each other so much. I hear in America there are many churches with people free to come and go as they please, but that on a nice day, you might choose to go on a picnic instead. We only have one Bible. We tore it up and divided it and each one memorized the portion they were given so we always have the words of God to share when we get together. Yet, I hear that Bibles are plentiful in America but that many Christians don't read them. Because of our suffering, we realize our need for God. I pray that you would see your need of God."

Pastor Tadessa saw our plenty, our comfort, and our freedom not as a blessing but as suffering because all of those "good" things were blinding our deepest need in life — God.

I would categorize this as a wake up call to **The Sin of INDIFFERENCE.** When we have everything we want, we don't pay much attention to God. We might be thankful, but we don't feel like we NEED Him. Not really. We think, *I got this.* As if we are just a bother to God to come to Him when we are not really in NEED. (Yet, we need Him in more ways than we know.) Can you imagine telling your spouse or kids they don't need to bother you unless they REALLY need something — but when they do you'll be there? That would be what a terrible father is like. God does not treat us that way. He wants to have a relationship with us EVERY day because everything is important when you're doing life with those you love. Yet, we don't treat God with the same affection or consideration.

Instead, we wonder why God allowed us to get fired, get sick, or get involved in something that drug us under. We can't believe that the natural disaster hit our home and spared the neighbors. Sometimes, God needs to get our attention — in hopes to put our affections and focus back where they belong.

Can you think of something that is going on now or has recently happened that forced you to pay attention to it?

If you wrote something down, talk to Jesus about that for a moment.

Look up Revelation 2:4 and 3:16.

What do you think Jesus is trying to get across in these verses?

Just like we'd expect our significant other to want us to be all-in, 100% committed to us and participating fully in our relationship, Jesus says the same. As time goes on, if we don't stay engaged in our relationship actively, things get less impactful, less meaningful, less important. Lacking. Lukewarm.

How is your relationship with Jesus? On the *Relationship Meter* below, mark where your relationship with Him is currently.

|____________________|____________________|

Indifferent   Intentional

Based on your answer, do you think God may be trying to get your attention because your relationship with Him is suffering?

If you are just starting your relationship with Jesus, let those verses be a warning to not let your love and your commitment to Him fade. If we don't make our relationship a priority that we care deeply about it won't be good. That leads us to another reason God may need to get your attention:
The sin of WRONG PRIORITIES.

It is easy to get sucked into the things of this world. In the U.S. we have all kinds of entertainment, activities, stuff to buy and enjoy, etc. Being interested in people and activities isn't bad unless those things start taking you away from what should be priorities for you. Ready to be honest? Write down your current priorities below. Remember, Jesus knows what they really are.

Write the 3 things you give most of your time, money, and attention to:

1.

2.

3.

If you don't know what the first of the 10 Commandments is, look it up in Exodus 20:3.

What is supposed to be your first priority?

We often think that things like sports, our jobs, or our kids don't qualify as being a "god" but our idols are anything we put ahead of God – that we value more than we value Him. Some justify not going to church because they have to work. They don't have time to read the Bible or pray because of a demanding family life. No time for God means you have other gods.

What happens when we don't put God first? Read 1 John 2:15-17.

What is going to happen to the things of the world? (v. 17)

What happens to those who do what God says? (v. 17)

God may be giving us a wake-up call because if He doesn't we won't make it. This life will be all there is for us. He wants us to be living with Him forever.

Talk this next exercise through with Jesus. In the margin, write down what you think a life of following Jesus looks like.

What do you think you'll miss out on NOW to be with Him FOREVER?

If I had to answer this question before I really started doing life with Him, I think I would have said (but not out loud!) something like, *"I'd probably have to give up anything fun, only do "religious" stuff, act "holy," and be really serious most of the time."* There is a myth that we all seem to believe, to some extent, that life with God isn't going to be as good as the life WE'D choose. Let me be the first one to tell you that is the biggest load of hogwash EVER!!!

The things we THINK we want are NOTHING compared to what God will show us. Doing things God's way will be EVERYTHING you never knew you wanted. The sooner you believe that truth, the quicker you'll be where you're meant to be.

I just recently came across this verse and thought it was amazing. Read 2 Corinthians 5:4 in the margin. Circle the last five words.

He's saying it's hard to be here, human with all our struggles, and while we don't want to die (or be dead like we were) we definitely want what's on the other side. We simply want to be swallowed up by life. The real life that awaits. The good news is that we don't have to wait until heaven for all of it if our attention is on Jesus. Focus on him and you'll be swallowed up by life.

Sit with Jesus. Talk to God

Ask Jesus how to turn your attention toward Him and put Him first. Listen.

For while we are in this tent, we groan and are burdened, because we do not wish to be unclothed but to be clothed instead with our heavenly dwelling, so that what is mortal may be swallowed up by life.
2 Corinthians 5:4

Day 2
BE REFINED

A GOOD POINT

Storms make trees take deeper roots.
-Dolly Parton

When I think about someone as being refined I guess my mind pictures an elegant lady wearing a very conservative lace dress with matching gloves. Her hair is perfectly coiffed and she is, of course, drinking tea with her pinky finger extended. Refined.

While being elegant and cultured is one definition, there are two others that fit what we are discussing today.

Definitions from Oxford Languages
Refined:

"developed or improved so as to be precise..."

"with impurities or unwanted elements having been removed..."

Not every hard thing that happens to us is because of blatant sin. Sometimes we are giving our full attention to God when the ground begins to quake. Get comfy with Jesus and answer the following questions.

Is there something going on in your life right now or in the recent past when you thought you were doing right by God and something hard occurred?

Talk to Jesus about that for a moment and jot down any thoughts.

Fire tests the purity of silver and gold, but the LORD tests the heart.
Proverbs 17:3 NLT

Let's see what God has to say about it. Read Zechariah 13:8-9

Who were the people God was going to refine?

"I will say, "They are __________ ______________." (v. 9)

Why would God do that? Read 1 Peter 1:6-7.

According to the Apostle Peter, why might we be experiencing something difficult? (v. 7)

Let's grab one more example. Read Malachi 3:2-4.

What was the benefit of being refined by God?

"Then the Lord will have men who will bring _____________ ____ _____________..." (v. 3)

To help put things in perspective let's find out a little more about what happens when silver is refined. There is a story that is told of a visit to a silversmith that explains a lot.

> A Bible study group was confused by the verse in Malachi 3:3. One of the members offered to learn about the process of refining silver and inform them at their next study. He visited a silversmith and watched him at work. The silversmith held a piece of silver over the fire and let it heat up. He explained that in refining silver you must hold the silver in the middle of the fire where the flames were hottest to burn away all the impurities. The member then thought about God holding us where the flames are the hottest to burn away our impurities. Then he thought again about the verse. *"And he shall sit as a refiner and purifier of silver."* He asked the silversmith if it was true that he had to sit there in front of the fire and watch the process. The silversmith answered that not only did he have to sit there holding the silver, but he had to keep his eyes on the silver the entire time it was "tested" in the fire. If the silver was left a moment too long in the flames, it would be destroyed. He explained you must leave it long enough to serve the purpose, but not too long as it would destroy it. The member was silent for a moment. Then asked the silversmith, "How do you know when silver is fully refined?" He smiled and answered, "Oh, that's easy — when I see my image in it."

God puts us through hard things to test our motives, our commitment, and to get rid of things that need to go. This is what transforms us into His image. As much as we might like to think we are good people we all have "dross" that needs to be burned off. Impurities. So often we are blind to these things because in "the world" we look okay. Society says we aren't arrogant but bold, we aren't selfish just busy, we're not prideful only confident. That stuff doesn't work when we are supposed to look like Jesus. Things need to change. As much as we might like to think we can humble ourselves to get there, in my experience, I haven't seen many people be successful at it without a little hardship in their lives.

People often don't want to believe that God could be the author of our life's hardest moments. But, just like a loving parent disciplines their child, this is part of our growing up process. If you are currently in the fire, it can be hard to know what is being "burned off." You may have to wait until it's over to know. Give some thought to this with Jesus and see what you hear.

What might be some things God needs to refine in you?

In the past or presently, have you experienced a hard time that helped you understand or change something in your life to make you a better person?

God is not the only one who can bring the refining fires to your life. Read Luke 22:31-32.

Who does Jesus say wants to "sift" Peter (aka Simon)?

Sifting would be in the same vein as refining — it's a painful process with a potentially similar result. Of course, the devil doesn't want to do if for the benefit of making you stronger or improved. He does it in the hope that you will not persevere. He wants you to give up, get bitter, walk away from God.

Go back and read verse 32 again.

What did Jesus say He would do for Peter?

What was going to be the outcome and the benefit?

And we know that in all things God works for the good of those who love him, who have been called according to his purpose.
Romans 8:28

Jesus KNEW Peter would make it because He'd taken care of it, and that Peter would be in a position to help the others once he got through it. Remember what Romans 8:28 tells us (see the margin if you need to refresh your memory).

One last question on Luke 22:31:

What did it say Satan did?

"Simon, Simon, Satan ________ __________ to sift all of you as wheat."

Be aware that Satan can do NOTHING to you without asking Jesus' permission. He will try to mess with us but he can do nothing without God being fully aware and on board with it. Satan is on a leash. A short one.

So why didn't Jesus just say no to Satan? Look up Matthew 16:18.

What important job was Jesus giving to Peter?

If you want to read any of the stories mentioned about Peter they are listed below.
Matthew 14:22-33
Luke 22:47-52
John 13:1-11
Luke 22:54-62

If you ask people who are living their lives like Jesus, being bold and making HIS agenda THEIR agenda, you'll likely find they have experienced Satan's sifting or a hard season of refining. If you read about Peter's life during his time with Jesus he is a fly-by-the-seat-of-your-pants kind of guy. He acts before he thinks. He was the one who jumped out of the boat to walk on water (and then sank), cut off a soldier's ear (and Jesus had to reattach it), told Jesus to wash his whole body (when Jesus wanted to wash his feet), and swore he'd die for Jesus (until that became a possibility and he lied that he even knew Him). Peter thought he was ready to be strong for Jesus but he had a lot to learn. When Jesus allows us to be sifted, it's because we need to learn something. Maybe a lot of things.

We may need to learn humility. Maybe how to be strong in the face of hard things. How to stop relying on ourselves, our family, our jobs, or our bank accounts and start relying on God. Only God. We may need to learn how to stop doing life alone. How to ask for help. How to give up control. How to have compassion. How to love, be patient, content, or quiet. How to be bold. Whatever it is, if you stick it out with God, you will learn it.

Perhaps James 1:2-4 explains it best. *"Consider it pure joy, my brothers and sisters, whenever you face trials of many kinds, because you know that the testing of your faith produces perseverance. Let perseverance finish its work so that you may be mature and complete, not lacking anything."*

Not everyone will go through difficult refining and Jesus does not allow Satan to refine everyone. Only if it's beneficial. However, we are told to be on guard and aware of Satan's presence in our world and what he's up to. Read 1 Peter 5:8.

What does it say the devil is looking for?

The Bible describes Satan as always accusing us (Rev. 12:10), a thief wanting to steal, kill, and destroy us (John 10:10). He is not only a liar but the father of lies (John 8:44). Perhaps his most cunning trick is that he masquerades as an angel of light (2 Cor. 11:14) – in other words he makes things look really good that are actually a nightmare. He is after ALL of mankind and will try to keep us or draw us away from God. If he can't do that he'll try to slow us down or stop us from being effective for the Kingdom. This is what is known as spiritual warfare.

Remember in Ephesians 6:12 we read that we are at war with evil spiritual forces. The good news is, while the devil will try to mess with us, we have help. Read 1 John 4:4 and James 4:7.

What do you hear Jesus saying about Satan?

As long as you stay close to Jesus the devil can't do any damage and any hardship he creates will ultimately be used for good. Stuff is going to come our way because we need to get stronger, learn how to endure through anything, mature in our faith, and be perfected. When the hard stuff comes, or if the fire is burning hot right now, look intently at the Silversmith's face and stick it out until you reflect His image.

Sit with Jesus. Talk to God

Talk to Jesus about what needs to be refined in your life. If you are not currently in a hard season, ask if there's a way to skip the refiner's fire. Otherwise, ask Him to help you understand how to endure it in a way that leaves you bright and shiny.

Day 3

ANSWERING PRAYER

A GOOD POINT

Sometimes when things are falling apart
they may actually be falling into place.
-Unknown

As I was talking over today's study with God, I was trying to figure out how to describe the gist of this lesson. Here's what I landed on: **Just because something bad is going on doesn't mean it's something bad.** After our last two days of study, maybe that's making a little sense. Let me have some people I know tell you about how hard things came as a result of prayers and why it wasn't a bad thing at all.

Teri had grown up like many — part button-down religious input plus some examples of being more wild and carefree. Trying to find herself, she experimented with drinking and drugs. When her high school boyfriend died in a car accident she learned to numb the pain with those things. Throughout college she continued the drugs and partying, yet quit when she found she was pregnant. She married. She thought she was in control. She wasn't. After the baby arrived she started chasing drugs again and denied she had a problem. Eventually, her husband left and her son went to live with grandparents. She had to admit she was a full-blown addict.

An abusive relationship followed. When she left him she went to meth to deaden the pain. Soon she was arrested and spent nine months in prison. When she got out she started drinking instead. It was three years before she went back to meth. She was proud of how long she'd been able to stay off of it. Shortly after, she met a new guy who was great — except that he cooked drugs. She was in love so she began helping him. She would later see that as *"the beginning of the end."*

> In June 2009, I met the feds for the first time. They arrested my boyfriend, but somehow let me go. He was facing 20 years to life. I got a call at 1 a.m. from his sister. He'd hung himself in his jail cell. I let go of hope in that moment.

Teri fell into a dark hole doing more and more drugs. When she found herself pregnant once again she was able to quit until his birth, but after, she went right back and found she couldn't stop.

> I knew that I was going to have DHS or the feds show up at any minute but I couldn't stop. I hated myself and I begged God to help me. God did. The feds kicked in my door in July 2012. I was indicted for conspiracy to distribute meth. I was looking at up to 20 years.

Don't worry, we'll come back to Teri, but first meet Janet and Todd.

They married later in life. They'd each done a lot of living, experiencing the ups and downs of life. When they met, they knew they'd found the right one. Janet had followed Jesus since she was a child and experienced Him deeply when she went through a difficult time. Todd hadn't grown up with that, but when he attended Janet's church he found it an awesome experience and started going every week.

As time went on they had some experiences that made it clear that God was moving in their lives and they wanted more. Their church had an opportunity to go to Israel and they signed up.

> The month before the trip, the sermon was 'pray to be broken so that you will learn to rely on God.' I did NOT pray that! Do I look like the kind of guy that would pray that?

Before they left, each did separately say a private prayer for their trip.

> Janet: I prayed that God would draw us closer together as a couple.
> Todd: That God would bring the Bible to life for me.

As they landed in Israel with the group, they had no idea how their prayers would take shape. The first day there, Todd's neck and back started hurting. It got so bad he went to the emergency room that night. After two days of suffering, and an intervention by an American doctor on their tour, he was diagnosed with spinal meningitis — a life-threatening condition. The tour was over for them. Todd was informed he must be quarantined in the Jerusalem hospital for the next 20 days. Their trip was supposed to be over in 10. The rest of their group had to move on the next day.

We'll circle back to our stories in a bit. First let's see what God has to say about our prayers. Read each verse below, then circle how the people approached God. Next underline what God says He will do. I've done the first one for you.

Psalm 34:17-18
"The righteous cry out and the Lord hears them; he delivers them from all their troubles. The Lord is close to the brokenhearted and saves those who are crushed in spirit."

Psalm 55:16-17
"As for me, I call to God, and the Lord saves me. Evening, morning and noon I cry out in distress, and he hears my voice."
Isaiah 65:24
"Before they call I will answer; while they are still speaking I will hear."
Jeremiah 29:12-13;
"Then you will call on me and come and pray to me, and I will listen to you. You will seek me and find me when you seek me with all your heart."
Lamentations 3:55-57
"I called on your name, Lord, from the depths of the pit. You heard my plea: 'Do not close your ears to my cry for relief.' You came near when I called you, and you said, 'Do not fear.'"
Matthew 6:6
"But when you pray, go into your room, close the door and pray to your Father, who is unseen. Then your Father, who sees what is done in secret, will reward you."
1 John 5:14-15
"This is the confidence we have in approaching God: that if we ask anything according to his will, he hears us. And if we know that he hears us—whatever we ask—we know that we have what we asked of him."

Circle which scripture above speaks loudest to you. Tell Jesus why.

For those who belong to God, we are assured that He hears us whether we ask, pray, call to Him or cry out. Day after day, God is answering our prayers, and often we don't even notice. I heard a little "funny" that showcases our lack of recognizing God's intervention in our lives.

> An elderly man was driving up and down the rows of the mall parking lot during the holiday season in hopes of finding a space close to the entrance. After several laps he prayed for God to help him find a spot. As he rounded the next row a car vacated the space that was closest to the doors. The man smiled and said, "Never mind, I've got one."

God does not usually answer our prayers in hard ways, but there are times when a difficult process delivers a more meaningful or long-term answer. To understand what I mean let's follow up with our stories –

Teri knew she wouldn't be able to stay sober while she was on pretrial release so she checked herself and her son into a treatment facility and everything was about to change. They helped her begin accepting responsibility for her life. She went to a Celebrate Recovery meeting each week as well.

I thought, "God can help me. I can't do it but He can!"

> I cried during the whole worship. I thought, "God can help me. I can't do it but He can!" I committed my life to Him and accepted Jesus

> in February 2013. I started to go to church. I worked my treatment program like it was life or death. I learned how to actually be a mom.
>
> I was blessed with an amazing Christian lawyer who somehow heard about my case. Instead of 20 years, I was sentenced to 24 months in federal prison.
>
> In there, I had no control over anything. I spent my time in treatment learning how to change my thinking and in the Bible learning how to change my heart. Everything changed.

Teri's life continued to change in the years that followed her release. She met Jose who had a very similar tale of death, destruction, addiction, and prison...and finding God. They married and today live happy lives with their sons. They oversee the Celebrate Recovery program at their local church, often working with addicts they knew – being a light to lives in darkness.

> Deuteronomy 30:3 in the Message Bible says, *"God your God, will restore everything you lost; he'll have compassion on you; he'll come back and pick up the pieces from all the places where you were scattered."* Truly, when God says He will "*restore*" it is so much more. I have never had this complete and full feeling in my life. And if you asked me what I could imagine I would never have imagined this!

God's answer to Teri's prayer was initially hard, but ultimately effective, utterly amazing, and joy producing.

What about our couple? Janet admitted she was scared the first couple of days.

> There were a few times he looked so bad, I thought he was going to die. I went to the bathroom and just sobbed, pleading with God for Todd.

He survived. During those 20 days, Janet stayed in the Old City in a convent. Many things were a challenge simply because they were not like the U.S. There was often a language barrier, the hospital was surrounded by barbed wire and armed guards were at the entrance, only the absolute basics were provided and even trying to make a call to the insurance company would take hours. They decided to make the best of their predicament.

Before Janet left the convent each morning she'd pray.

> I asked for God to put someone in my path that day that would help me and that I could also help. I had the most amazing taxi drivers. They were so kind and compassionate when I shared our story. One drove me to the hospital by way of an overlook so I could see the view of the vast desert. I'd have these little mini adventures on the way to the

> hospital so I'd have something to share with Todd. It was one of the most painful and scary times, but God placed people on my path that were able to help and give me hope. God answered my prayer and put me in situations where I could show compassion to someone. I was listening to His whispers and nudges and then acting on them.

Over the coming days Janet helped an elderly woman carry groceries, took tea to a woman who's husband was also in the hospital and very ill. Janet brought in food and snacks for Todd and his roommate to share. People often looked in their room as they passed by. They found out from the staff that the people found them very interesting — standing out among the local Jews and Muslims. One afternoon, an old man walked in and sat on the end of Todd's bed and began speaking in Hebrew. Todd's roommate said the man wanted them to pray for him to be healed. They prayed and he left.

> Prayer is remarkable. We knew how grateful we were for the people back home who were praying for us during that time.

I knew whatever happened, this was going to be His plan. Once I believed that, things got easier...

As Todd healed, Janet continued to make the days special by coming up with themes for each day like "Art Day" where they toured the hospital halls looking at the art on the walls or "Behind the Scenes" where they explored the hospital grounds and learned where supplies were if they wanted to make tea. After 20 days, everything came together for them to be able to leave — including the miracle of finding a nurse to fly home with them. Todd reflected.

> I never thought I was going to die, but God broke me in Israel. I was always someone who thought I could handle anything at anytime. God showed me that I couldn't handle and control things. I thought of that sermon — I learned I needed to rely on God. I knew whatever happened, this was going to be His plan. Once I believed that, things got easier in Israel. I knew God had a plan for me and that He will always be by my side.

What better way to see the Bible come alive (Todd's prayer) than to profoundly know that God is going to take care of your life? And Janet's prayer?

> The funny thing is that I prayed that Todd and I would have time alone together. Prayers are answered but not always in the fashion you think they will be.

Sit with Jesus. Talk to God

What prayers have you had hard answers to? Talk to Jesus about how you might be missing out on blessings if you've ever felt bitter about difficult answers. Look back on times you prayed and things seemed to get worse and see if there was something good that you're overlooking. Work through it with God.

Day 4
IT'S PERSONAL

A GOOD POINT

Even before there is a word on my tongue,
Behold, O Lord, You know it all.
-Psalm 139:4 NASB

For those of us in the United States — or anywhere people can enjoy life, freedom, and worship without hindrance — somewhere along the way we were lied to — or perhaps we just assumed wrongly. Here's how it goes: *If I am good with God, have accepted Jesus as my Savior, then my life will be good. Period. If it's not, something is wrong with my faith. God's mad at me.* I have absolutely believed that lie.

I remember hearing a preacher one time profess something to the effect of *"Jesus suffered so we won't have to."* Apparently, her season of refining had not yet happened. I have heard other believers say things like, *"If you believe enough your [cancer, addiction, struggle] will go away."* No pressure there. And even more head-shakingly-sad, those who have said or implied to someone who lost a loved one to illness, *"You must not have believed enough."*

There is just one word for all those thoughts: Garbage. In our society where everything good is our goal, our biggest question in times of trouble and uncertainty is often, *"Why me?"* (or *Why my child, my parent, my spouse?*) In countries where they are not afforded freedoms, when bad things happen they do not cry out with a question, but a plea: *"Help me!"* Talk to Jesus and ask Him to help you write down how your response could alter your thoughts.

Thoughts when you think:
Why me?

In the margin, write what thoughts you might have if you ask God, WHY ME? vs. if you cry, HELP ME!

We've looked at many of the things that the Apostle Paul went through. Let's look at a couple other things in his life you might find VERY interesting. Read these three passages in Acts: 14:8-10, 19:11-12, and 20:7-12.

List the different ways Paul was able to heal people.

What's different when you cry:
Help me!

God gifted Paul in amazing ways. It was almost as if he couldn't help but heal people. However... Look up 2 Timothy 4:20 and answer the question below.

What is the condition of Paul's ministry partner Trophimus?

Now, look up Philippians 2:25-27.

Does this sound like one of Paul's miraculous healings? Why or why not?

Two of Paul's close ministry partners, serving God, were sick. And God didn't heal them — at least not right away. The Bible doesn't tell us why these particular men suffered, but Paul himself had a problem that gives us some insight into the sufferings of believers. Look up 2 Corinthians 12:6-10.

What was Paul's problem? (v. 7)

How many times did he ask God to take it away? (v. 8)

Why did God allow it? (v. 7)

"Therefore, in order to keep me from _________ ___________."

Instead of saying, "No," to Paul's request, what did God say?

In light of what Paul says in response in verses 9 and 10, sit with Jesus and let Him talk to you about what that means. Write your thoughts below.

How are we strong when we are weak?

Hard things can come into our lives because God knows us so well. It's personal with God. Paul had an incredible encounter with Jesus on the road to Damascus, one that changed him forever. After that, God gave him the ability to heal people so that they would see God was with him, that Jesus he told them about WAS the Savior. He saw people give their lives to Christ. He suffered through many things, but in all of it he saw God at work — rescuing, healing, opening doors, offering escape. He saw that it wasn't him (Paul), but God who could make things happen. Yet, because Paul was given so much revelation, and because God knew Paul's character, He knew it would go to his head if he didn't keep him in check, so He allowed him to have a problem. While no one knows for sure what the "thorn" was, it was likely a physical issue, something that would keep him humble.

Paul wasn't bitter that he wasn't healed, instead he rejoiced because he knew how he had been before he met Jesus. He knew he never wanted to be like that again and was happy to admit that he couldn't do it on his own. He was glad that God cared enough to do what needed doing to keep Paul in the right mindset to fully appreciate what God had done, through Jesus, to save him.

Coming to God with a *Why Me?* mindset can leave us feeling like a victim instead of a beloved child of God. Yet, asking *Why Me?* isn't necessarily bad as long as you are willing to listen. Paul assumed his hard thing needed to go, but when he listened to God he found out why it was allowed and that it's residence in his life was going to benefit him. Maybe more helpful is taking issues to God with a *Help Me!* approach. That takes the accusation out of it and instead positions us to look at Our Father as Our Helper as His Word details He is.

God knows us so well that He will allow and orchestrate things that help us on our unique journey, to mold us into the distinct source of blessing He has planned. What Paul went through won't be your story. Your blessings and your "thorns" will be all YOURS.

Before I send you off with Jesus to talk about some things, I need to cover one more important item. God DOES NOT use things like addictions, abuse, or mental health issues as your "thorn!" Nor will He keep you fearful or burdened with worry. These go against His promises. Nothing sinful will be your thorn. These are not from God.

What God knows about me based on Psalm 139

Our God is a personal God. Read through Psalm 139 with Jesus. In the margin, write down all the different things that God knows about you.

How does knowing what God knows about you make you feel?

Which of those things gives you the most comfort?

You are unique and special and what God will allow in your life will be absolutely what needs to be there to make sure you make it Home to Him. He takes your life personally.

Sit with Jesus. Talk to God

Have you, or are you, experiencing a "thorn" in your life? Remember, this isn't something sinful or what someone else is putting on your life. It might be (or was) a temporary sickness (not everything will be in your life "forever") or it may be an ongoing issue. Talk to Jesus about anything that may qualify and how you turn any *Why Me?* thinking into *That's For Me!* rejoicing. If nothing comes to mind, spend some time thinking about areas where you are weak right now, where you absolutely need to embrace God's strength. Rejoice in the realization that it can be a place of victory!

Day 5

GOD'S GOT A PLAN

A GOOD POINT

Anyone can sing a tune on a clear day at noon,
but God, give me a song at midnight.
-Attributed to an old hymn lyric

So far this week we've explored several reasons hard things happen in our lives. Probably the big question that remains is related to those hard things that just don't make any sense no matter how long or from what angle you look at them.

Why do helpless children suffer at the hands of adults? Why do people starve? Why are there so many diseases and disorders? Why are so many allowed to endure horrific things? Why doesn't God just step in and stop it all?

My mom and my mother-in-law were best friends. My mother was healthy and exercised each day, ate right, and was active in her church. VERY active. She was always on some board, serving others, and trying to help people meet Jesus. She was a great mom and a wonderful grandma. She was the force who kept us all together. On the day her life was cut short, she had walked her great-granddaughter to school and had supplies out on the counter to make a pie for church that night. She was living a full life.

In contrast, my mother-in-law had many health problems and had even lost her leg, suffered serious fallout from a long bout with cancer, and had to move to a nursing facility. All of these struggles restricted her ability to feel like she was contributing in any way that felt meaningful — as she had done in the past. When my mother died, my mother-in-law was devastated. She wept and openly questioned why God would take her healthy, productive friend instead of her. It made no sense to her.

Sit with Jesus. Is there something in your life (now or in the past) you just can't make sense of why God would allow it?

This past year, we had two different families in our church loose children to accidents. One family lost two on the same day. Most of us can't even process that kind of loss. When I was growing up, there was a very nice family in our church. Their daughter was a sweet girl who was very quiet. In her early adult years she had a mental breakdown. It came out that she'd been molested as a child for years by a family friend and felt she could never tell. I know two people who are currently awaiting sentencing in jail. One, in a fit of jealous rage killed someone they thought was messing with their significant other.

Another got together with an old flame to get high. One didn't live through it.

I think we can all agree that our world is broken. It's been that way since Adam and Eve allowed sin to be ushered in. Sin is a toxic state that makes us believe rebellion against God will get us something better.

Because humanity embraces sin we grow wicked. We think about ourselves, OUR desires, what will make US happy. We do what WE want at the expense of others. We take care of #1 — us. We think pursuing success and power and money will take us to the highest heights. We chase the desires of our flesh. That leaves untold carnage in its wake. List any of the evils of the world and you'll find these pursuits in full throttle. That's why children often become collateral damage. That's why relationships crumble. That's why families fall apart. That's why nations suffer.

One big reason things are so bad is stated in 1 John 5:19

Who does it say is in control?

What is he in control of?

If that's a little worrisome, read a little before and after that verse and exhale. 1 John 5:18 and 20.

Who does Jesus keep safe? (v. 18)

What does it say the evil one cannot do? (v. 18)

Even though Satan may be wreaking havoc in the world, read 1 John 4:4 in the margin, and see who trumps him.

Why don't you need to worry?

You, dear children, are from God and have overcome them, because the one who is in you is greater than the one who is in the world.
1 John 4:4

If the devil is doing so much harm in the world, pushing evil and chaos, why doesn't God just step in and stop it? Read 2 Peter 3:9.

What is God waiting for?

If God sweeps in right now there would be a LOT of people who are going to hell. How many people do you know today that wouldn't make it to heaven?

Write down those you know who haven't chosen to follow Jesus.

God, in His mercy and patience, is giving everyone time to figure it out. To turn away from sin and time to come to Him. Time to accept what Jesus has paid for. While we may never understand many things that happen in this world, realize that God IS ultimately in control and there is a plan. Read the verses on the following page and answer each question.

Psalm 139:16	How many days had you lived before God knew what would happen in every one of them?
Proverbs 19:21	Regardless of man's plans whose purpose is fulfilled?
Isaiah 14:24	How many of God's plans will work out?
Philippians 1:6	As a believer in Jesus, what is Paul sure of for you?

Remember Janet and Todd from our Day 3 study who went to Israel? You might think that was the pinnacle of their big God stories. It's not. They have had amazing encounters with God in SUCH interesting ways.

Janet had a surprising incident on a trip with a youth group to Haiti (we'll tell the story of the witch doctor's wife another time), they experienced God's intervention in an unplanned hosting of a foreign exchange student (resulting in a global friendship and a trip to Lithuania), and Todd served God on a team doing relief work after a flood in Texas — just to name a few. They were loving this life's adventure with God. And then there was the lump on Todd's arm.

It turned out to be Non-Hodgkin's Lymphoma. To be real, Janet lost it.

> We're human. I had a moment I was mad at God one day — just angry. I stood in my kitchen and cried, "WHY!" Here is my super strong husband and all that he's had to go through. But then, the next minute I'm thankful, realizing how full our life is.

When treatment began, Todd had an allergic reaction to one of the medications. It was so bad Janet had to leave the hospital room. She had some tears and a chat with God. When she was allowed back in, Todd was casually talking with the nurse, inviting her to church.

> Because I relied on God at the end of my Israel stay, I told Janet, "God's got this. It's going to be okay, regardless of how it comes out — whether I live or I don't. I just have great faith that God will be there to welcome me to heaven at the end. Whenever that is. And I feel great about that.
>
> It's pretty much constant, Him walking beside me. There have been days when I can't get out of bed, but God is there helping me. It's like that story...

Todd's eyes filled with tears, his voice filled with emotion as he finished...

> about the Footprints in the Sand. "Why did You leave me?" And He says, "I didn't leave you. That's when I carried you." That's what gets me. It's exactly that. He's never NOT there. I never lose trust in His plan.

If you are unfamiliar with *Footprints In The Sand* you can find it online and at Christian retailers.

Yep, it's a struggle for Janet at times. She doesn't want to lose her best friend. But she sums it up like this:

> We've just come to believe that no matter what, it's going to be okay, through Him.

What does Todd think will happen?

> I'm not sure. It's not my plan.
>
> I thank God for the journey I'm on — I've made friends, met Janet, have a great church, being able to tell my son and my daughter I love them. My cancer journey may not be about me at all. Maybe it's for someone else to learn from. I'll find out in heaven.

Life causes a ripple effect. When babies are born and when people die many lives are affected — some in good ways, some in bad. Like a tsunami, an earthquake in one part of the world can be devastating to others even thousands of miles away. While we can't always know what the outcome of hard things will be, we can trust that God has a plan.

When my mom died, it was unexpected. She was hit by a bus crossing the street. I had a co-worker who used to say, *"If I get hit by a bus, here's what you need to know..."* Turns out that actually happens sometimes. But when it happened to my mom, while it was shocking, I never questioned God about it. Not in anger anyhow. Psalm 121:4-5 came to mind.

Who never sleeps?
Who is always watching you?

There was not an, *"Oops!"* on God's part when my mom got hit. He didn't look away and tragedy struck. He knew what was going to happen and He swept her into His arms and off to heaven. That's the comfort that we as believers have. Here's another verse that I love. Read Psalm 55:16-18 and fill in the blank.

"He rescues me _________ from the battle waged against me," (v. 18)

In the end, no matter what has occurred here on planet Earth, for those who have turned to Jesus and are trusting in Him, we will enter heaven *unharmed.*

God just isn't going to explain everything to us. He simply tells us there's a plan for us to make it out of here eternally alive. An offer that's available to everyone. He encourages us to share that plan with the world. We just have to trust the plan. Look up John 13:7 and complete what Jesus tells us.

"You do not realize now what I am doing, but ________ ________ ________ ______________."

It isn't our job to figure it all out. We decided to follow Jesus because we believed He knew better how to run our lives than us. The same holds true for the world. We can worry and whine about our broken world or revel that God has a plan — one that we get to be part of.

Sit with Jesus. Talk to God

Share your thoughts with Jesus about today's lesson and how to trust God's plan.

Do the wrap up at the end of your week — perhaps on your Day 6. It's a good way to recap what you've learned all week and capture the things that were most important to you.

The Hard Road

WEEKLY WRAP UP

Write what point, quote, or Scripture stood out most to you this week

This week's memorization verse(s)

Memorize the verse you circled as the most meaningful to you on Day 3. (Pgs. 113-114)

Hey! Are you ready to get off the hard road? I may have prayed about this past week's study more than any of the other ones. There are so many different reasons for hard things in our lives from the workings of evil, our bad choices, and straight up living in a broken world to lessons from God and seasons of maturing. I think many of us have been duped into thinking it's supposed to be so comfy here — that bad things shouldn't happen to us. We need to remember it's not heaven. Here's a good analogy I heard once:

> A man boarded a plane and was told to just sit back and relax and that everything would be fine on his trip. He would be comfortable and everything would be taken care of. The stewardess told him that he should wear a parachute for added protection. As the flight progressed, the parachute became uncomfortable and he complained to the stewardess. She assured him it was for his safety. He endured it awhile longer but was noticing other troubles. His food wasn't what he expected, the person in the next seat annoyed him, the plane was quite stuffy, and he was not as comfortable as they had promised. In time, he became so annoyed and uncomfortable that he threw off his parachute in an attempt to achieve some level of comfort.
>
> Another man who boarded the same flight was told by his stewardess that the ride could be bumpy and that he should wear the parachute in the likely event that they would need to jump from the plane at a moment's notice. The man happily strapped on the parachute, knowing it was his only salvation. He didn't expect the ride to be comfortable, but instead embraced the safety and security he felt having the parachute. Because his focus was on being prepared to leave the plane, he rather enjoyed the food and the company of the other passengers. He was kind to them knowing they were all on this precarious journey together.
>
> During the flight, one of the stewardesses brought hot coffee around. Turbulence sent her flying with a hot pot of coffee in hand which splashed the two men. The one who had expected a comfortable flight was furious and it only added to his discontentment and discouragement. The other man quickly recovered from the situation and was just all the more ready for the moment to depart the flight...his attention fully on the salvation of the parachute.

Jesus is our parachute. The plane is this life on earth. I don't know who the author is of that analogy, but it's a good reminder of John 16:33, *"In this life you will have trouble."* This is why you need Jesus. When we accept Jesus it's easy for us to think that now all troubles will cease. And as Christians, we have often perpetuated this myth. When we don't expect bad things to happen, we don't know how to handle it when they do. We get all sorts of bad feelings – often toward God. When hard things happen, that is when we need to cling to Our Savior the most. He will help us get through all the turbulence of our lives and he'll be with us when we depart this flight. We can't make the leap without him.

For those of you trying to navigate your way through something incredibly difficult, I feel your pain. You just want it to be over. You just want to be "normal." When I was going through my hardest time, I would have traded anyone what they were going through – certain that my suffering was the worst kind of all. I felt that way because I thought there was no fixing it. There was no light at the end of the tunnel, only more darkness.

If you feel similarly, let me tell you that it absolutely WILL work out. It will get better! With God, your hard season will blow over and a time of refreshing is coming. Things will change, and YOU will change. In the wake of the hard things, as you're battered upon the rocks, you will become different. Just like stones that are polished become beautiful, so will your life and your story with God. God does not fail! Your job is to hang on tight to Him, lean in to listen and to learn as you walk the hard road. In time, you'll come to a path so lovely you'll see that finding it will outshine all the darkness.

Taking stock: Answer the questions below to process this week's study.

What were some key things that you felt Jesus nudging you about this week?

What was the most positive thing you felt Jesus wanted you to hear this week?

Sit with Jesus. Talk to God

Review the week with Jesus. Write a prayer to God that expresses your journey on the hard road. Tell Him what's hardest about it and where you need His help. Finish by committing to His plan and process, and asking for patience and perseverance to travel the hard road well.

Knowing Jesus Tip:

When I was in the hardest fight of my life, I often couldn't sleep because my mind couldn't stop worrying and processing the difficulties. Instead of lying there feeling overwhelmed and fearful, I learned to just get up and get with God. I'd read the Bible, pray, sometimes cry, admit my fears, failures, and doubts. I'd read the help notes in my study Bible. If there was another verse referenced, I'd read that too. I used it as a time of learning. I have friends who put their earbuds in and listen to Christian music or let the Bible app read scripture while they go back to sleep. Fight back. Spend time with Jesus, not your dark thoughts.

WEEK 6

BEING DIFFERENT

Most of us would agree that if we ate right and exercised we'd lose weight. If I believe that is true, but never do those things, what changes on the scale? Nothing. The same concept is true for our faith. If all we do is continue to say what we believe, instead of behaving in a way that owns it, nothing will change for us. So, so, many Christians are stuck in this reality — speaking beliefs instead of living them — so nothing's different.

This week is where the rubber meets the road. We have to start the DOING of our faith. The OWNING of God's promises. The LIVING out the life of a Jesus follower. This is truly where everything goes from head-knowledge to life-change. It's time to be different.

Photo: Belle Collective . Unsplash.com

Day 1
HOW TO CHANGE

A GOOD POINT

Sometimes when you're in a dark place you think you've been buried, but actually you've been planted.
-Christine Caine

When I was a kid, people would say, *"You're so skinny you'd blow away in a strong wind!"* A decade or so later, after the birth of my children, I was putting on a few pounds and I didn't like it. I realized I needed to do something. I started getting up early in the morning in order to do a 30-minute workout that was on TV Monday through Friday (this was before the days of DVRs and streaming). I also had to change my eating habits. Some foods had to go. I gave up the big glass of milk with supper, started watching my portions, and learned how to eat well. Thirty years later, I still exercise every day (nearly) and watch what I eat (mostly). I have never regretted those decisions. But change isn't easy. It costs us something.

In order to be fit and healthy today, I had to sacrifice. I sacrificed some sleep, time, some pleasure (sorry Twinkies®), and some comfort. Learning to be different was uncomfortable while I learned to eat different, shop different, cook different, and embrace a different schedule. But, I was motivated because doing those things got me the results I wanted. What results do you want in your life? Sit with Jesus and see what comes to your mind today.

Tell Jesus what is motivating you to be different.

The way we become different in how we think, feel, act, respond to the world, and treat ourselves and others starts with one big action. Read Matthew 16:24-26.

What does Jesus tell us to do?

Let's make sure we understand what He's getting at. Read the verses below.

Colossians 3:3
For you died, and your life is now hidden with Christ in God.

Mark 8:35
For whoever wants to save their life will lose it, but whoever loses their life for me and for the gospel will save it.

Galatians 2:20
I have been crucified with Christ and I no longer live, but Christ lives in me.

Who needs to die?

YOU need to die. We're not talking about taking your *physical* life, you need to lay down your *inner* life. You need to die to SELF. You have to put to death all your plans, expectations, and desires. You have to walk away from your ideas about what will make you happy, what you think will make you feel good, and what you want in life. You have to walk away from being in control. That's what *repentance* means. I love how Wikipedia defines it –

Metanoia is the Greek word for repentance.

God as Sovereign: Having total control and absolute authority.

Wikipedia

Repentance

The doctrine of repentance as taught in the Bible is a call to persons to make a radical turn from one way of life to another. **The repentance (metanoia) called for throughout the Bible is a summons to a personal, absolute and ultimate unconditional surrender to God as Sovereign.** Though it includes sorrow and regret, it is more than that. It is a call to conversion from self-love, self-trust, and self-assertion to obedient trust and self-commitment to now live for God and his purposes.

Following Jesus is costly. It will cost you your life everyday.

Following Jesus is costly. It will cost you your life everyday. Don't let that scare you. We're not giving up our lives to an evil ruler. We are giving up our lives to follow The One who created us, The One who IS love, The One who gave His life for us, The One who adopted us as His own, The One who wants us to be with Him forever. The One who knows precisely what we need in our lives to make us feel loved, fulfilled, complete, joyful, and at peace.

Look up Mark 10:17-22 and fill in the blank.
"Jesus looked at him and loved him. "One thing you lack," he said. "Go, sell ________________ you have..."

Giving up our lives means giving up everything. From the rich man, Jesus asked him to give up what was most important in his life. Notice Jesus told the man to give up everything AND THEN come follow Him.

Luke 14:33 says, *"In the same way, those of you who do not give up everything you have cannot be my disciples."* Jesus tells each of us to give up everything so that we can follow Him.

Tell Jesus what you are freaking out about right now.

Does Jesus really want us to sell everything we own? Maybe. But probably not. What He's getting at is we need to be in a mindset that puts Him in front of EVERYTHING else in our lives. If He wants you to quit your job you do it.

If He tells you to breakup with the one you've been dating, or seeing on the side, you do it. If you know you shouldn't be doing that thing that you always do, you stop doing it. If He tells you to give to the poor, even when you need a new car, you do it. You stop considering what YOU want and start focusing on what HE wants.

Do you know what freedom there is to dying to yourself? When we die to self we'll stop over-analyzing our lives. We can take a break from wondering why we feel this way or that, why we don't have what our friends have, who we should date or marry, why we're depressed, if things will go this way or that. **If you spent your time focused on Jesus instead of yourself, what would you be free from?** As you tell Jesus, write down some things you'd like to stop focusing on.

What will you feel free from? (What do you find yourself obsessing over about your physical self, your life, your inner being?)

Until we get ourselves out of the way we will miss one big thing we need to do as Christians. Jesus exampled it well. Look up John 6:38.

"For I have come down from heaven, not to do _____ _____, but to do _____ _______ _______ _______ who sent Me."

Everything Jesus did was to point people to God. That's how we're supposed to live. If we want a life that is different we have to get over ourselves. Our healing, our confidence, our restoration WILL happen when we focus on Jesus and learn to be like Him — always living for God.

We've talked about the Apostle Paul quite a bit. In certain circles he was called Saul. If you aren't familiar with how he started following Jesus, it happened on the road as he was headed to Damascus. At the time, Jesus had recently been crucified, and Jesus' disciples and followers were telling everyone about His resurrection and the good news that they could be saved and their relationship with God restored.

Paul was part of the Jewish leadership — the Pharisees. They were the ones responsible for getting Jesus crucified. (He was rocking their lifestyle boat and making them look foolish. Plus, He kept telling them that they were a problem and not the solution they thought they were.) They wanted to snuff out any remaining loyalism to Jesus' following (known as The Way). Remember, Paul had previously been party to killing at least one Christian. He was not a nice guy.

Read Acts 9: 1-22 to hear his encounter with Jesus.

What was Paul (Saul) going to Damascus to do? (v. 2)

What one question did Paul ask Jesus? (v. 5)

What did Paul do after he got his sight and his strength back? (v. 20)

When Paul met Jesus his whole life changed. He gave up everything once he realized who Jesus REALLY was. His encounter with Jesus was so powerful he walked away from his family, friends, his way of life, his career, and his power and authority without hesitation. Within days he went from being part of the Jewish "in" crowd to being an outcast. He didn't care. Knowing Jesus meant everything to him.

Take one more look at verse 18.

What else did Paul do after he could see?

Theology professor Randy Harris puts it this way –

> Baptism is saying, "I'm all in!" It's the confession that there is nothing you can do and casting yourself on the mercy of God. You can either be in control or give it all up.

He goes on to explain that there was a moment when Jesus gave up His control. He could call on the angels to save Him from death and hell but He relinquished control to God the Father – thereby saving us. That same act of letting go of control is evidenced in our baptism.

If you haven't been baptized, do it. Jesus tells us to do it. It's the stamp on the acceptance of Christ in your life that says I'm giving it all up for Jesus. I'm all in!

To be honest, my exercise and eating plan didn't happen overnight. It took time to let some things go and embrace new things. Your journey with Jesus will likely take some time as well. Somethings will be obvious that need to go (like my Twinkies). Other things will come to your attention later. The key is to keep letting things come in and go out as Jesus shows them to you. In order to change your life, your first job is to wake up everyday and die to yourself. Then, smile at Jesus and ask Him where He's taking you today. What I gave up to get what I wanted doesn't feel like a sacrifice today. It's a blessing. Welcome to different!

Sit with Jesus. Talk to God

Just talk to God about the things that are hard for you to let go of and ask Him how you do that. Pray about your fears, reservations, and excitement around dying to yourself. Note what things He's telling you now.

Day 2

MAKE A DECISION

A GOOD POINT

To live is the rarest thing in the world. Most people exist, that is all.
-Oscar Wilde

Dying to self each day is a necessary step to get to where we want to be. Two other steps follow closely. Let's see if you can determine what the first one is from a story in the Bible about a crippled man who spent his days near a sacred pool. The pool was reported to have healing powers, but only when "the waters stirred" and only for the first one who got in when that happened. Read John 5:1-9 to see what happens, then answer the question below.

What did Jesus ask the man (v. 6)

Talk to Jesus about why He asked Him that.

If you struggled answering the last one, maybe this will help. A friend of mine, Shelli, works with at-risk teens and adults. For many she works with they start doing well and improving in a lot of ways. They make goals and start moving toward them. And then…

Shelli: You said you wanted to get a job. I know a place that is hiring.
Woman: Oh. But I don't have a way to get there.
Shelli: What about riding the bus? Doesn't it stop just down the block?
Woman: I don't think their hours would work for me.

This is when it dawns on Shelli that she forgot to ask the question: *Do you want to get well?* As an addict in recovery, Shelli knows the excuses game well and has seen how they lead to the undoing of ourselves again and again. One thing she says you have to decide is what you want and then remember YOU picked it. Then, to make RATIONAL decisions accordingly.

> If what you want is to get high, then it's totally rational to drive to the drug dealer's house. However, if you want to be a good mom, than that idea [of going to the drug dealer] is completely irrational. You have to know what you want and then act in ways to get what you want. You can't be ambivalent – you can't have both things (though the devil will try to convince you you can). You have to determine whether what you are doing is taking you TOWARD or AWAY from your long-term goals.
>
> When the excuses start, I remind them of what THEY said they wanted.

Any thoughts now as to why Jesus asks us, *"Do you want to be well?"*

Pastor Gene has a ministry that works with men dealing with serious life struggles. Once the man determines what goals he is after and they discuss the steps they'll take to achieve the goals, Pastor Gene has them sign a contract of sorts agreeing that this is THEIR plan and that they are committing to do what it takes.

> I put the paper in front of them, hand them a pen, and give them the option, "You are a grown man. You have the choice to do this or not. Make a decision. Sign this and be all-in or don't and walk away. But, if you sign it, remember it was your choice."

Sometimes, we want to "be well" right until things get hard. Jesus, asking us if we want to be well, asks us to consider the cost. For the man who had done life at the pool for 38 years, begging and relying on others, being healed would mean a MAJOR life change. He'd have to get a job, start doing things for himself, maybe step up and show up for those who'd cared for him for so long. Jesus was truly asking if he was ready for this life change.

Over the last few weeks you've identified some areas that need to change in your life. That YOU want to be different. So, given YOUR situation, are you ready to have a changed life? Sit for a bit with Jesus and talk about what this looks like for you, then answer Jesus' question.

Write down some things that will change if you are "well."

Do you want to be well?

I pray your answer was yes. If so, and you're not only going to *Die To Yourself*, but you also *Want To Be Healed*, another item that is key is something that can sneak up on you. Let's see if you can uncover the next step in the following Bible story.

To read more about the **Ark of the Covenant** see Exodus 25: 10-22.

God was about to make good on a promise He had made to His chosen people. They were going to go take possession of lands that other nations occupied. As you can imagine, that would be unnerving to say the least. Not only that, they'd have to cross the Jordan River to get there and at this time of year it was at flood stage. And, they were carrying the most holy thing on earth, the *Ark of the Covenant*. This was a wooden box covered in gold that held the 10 Commandments and other God-given items, and it was where God's presence resided when it was in the temple. In order for God to show them that He was with them He was about to wow them. Read Joshua 3:7-17.

How were they able to cross the river?

When did the water stop flowing? (v. 15)

Our transformation takes our COOPERATION. It will happen when we are in motion, not going through the motions. The water didn't part UNTIL their feet were wet.

Too often, those who claim to be Christ followers are just *flockers*. We go to church on Sunday with everybody else, we get involved in church activities because we're supposed to, we might even participate in a group Bible study because our friends are. Those things are great, but for many that is the end of the road with Jesus. That's not following Jesus, that's flocking with friends.

Showing up at church is something anyone can do. Showing up to spend time privately with your Savior is only something the devoted will do.

Showing up at church is something anyone can do. Showing up to spend time with your Savior privately is only something the devoted will do.

Years ago, I used to go to a health club where the program relied on a circuit of machines. Each machine targeted a different area of your body. In about half-an-hour, members could move from one machine to another, getting a full-body workout. The problem was, most of the members just went through the motions letting the equipment do the work. They chatted with their friends on the adjacent machines and had a good time, but in the end, few saw any worthwhile results. They forgot what their purpose was — not just to be with their friends, but to finally see changes in themselves.

Christ didn't call us to go to church, He called us to go to God. He called us to a changed life — and for those who know they need that change, that's ultimately why we gave our lives to Jesus. We WANT that change.

Let's take a look at one more Bible story to see what happens to those who show up for the party, but who don't want to change. Read Matthew 22:1-13.

What was the king's complaint about the man? (vs. 11-12)

Back in those days, people invited to such a wedding would be provided special attire to wear by the host. Yet, for some reason, the man decided not to change.

What does Jesus say happened to the man? (v. 13)

Jesus is warning us. If you want to be part of the party, there's no other way to experience the goodness without change. Yet, the choice is yours. When you make the decision to *die to yourself*, to *be well*, and to *be actively participating in changing*, things will change, and both you and The King will smile.

Sit with Jesus. Talk to God

Review the Good Point at the top of today's lesson and talk to Jesus about your decisions today and how to stay committed so you can experience the change — to truly live and not merely exist.

Day 3

FROM FEAR TO POWER

A GOOD POINT

It's not faith you need, it is faith in a great God.

-N.T. Wright

Hi. How are you doing this week? I know we're getting to the end of our study and I'm thinking about you a lot. I wonder if you are feeling joyful, stronger, and more hopeful than when we started this journey. Oh how much I pray that you are having some incredible times of experiencing Jesus and KNOWING that God is with you!

Today's lesson is a biggie for us to learn so we can live it out and eliminate fear in our lives and feel strength in our souls. First, just to recap the last two lessons, try to write from memory what three things you need to do in order to be different and have a changed life.

1. Each day I'm going to _____ to myself.
2. I have decided I want to be ______.
3. I know I need to be actively ________________ in changing.

Now, let's turn our minds to today's task – learning how to move from fear to living a powerful life. A couple of weeks ago, we defined our worries and fears and started working on eliminating those life-drainers and time-wasters. Because this is such a common thing in our lives on a number of levels, we're going to add to our insight and arsenal. To start, we are going to look at two very different individuals in the Bible and their approach to fear.

First, let's check in on David. Everybody wants to be a David. When David was just a boy, tending his family's flocks, God's prophet told his father that David was the next chosen king of Israel. As a young man he was strong, good-looking, didn't seem to care what others thought, and he was fearless.

When a conflict broke out between the Israelites and the Philistines, David's brothers went to fight. David had other responsibilities at home and serving King Saul, but his father Jesse sent him with some food for his brothers and to check on how they were doing. He finds out that a giant of a warrior named Goliath has thrown down a challenge – *"Choose a man and have him come down to me. If he is able to fight and kill me, we will become your subjects; but if I overcome him and kill him, you will become our subjects and serve us."* (1 Samuel 17:8-9) King Saul and all the Israelites were terrified. For weeks Goliath came out each day to fight, waiting for them to send someone to face him. Read 1 Samuel 17:22-26 and 32-50 to see how David reacted.

How did King Saul see David? (v. 33)

How does David refer to himself? (v. 34)

Who did David credit with saving him from the bear and the lion? (v. 37)

What did David "come against" Goliath with to defeat him? (v. 45)

Now, let's take a look at David's opposite: Gideon. He too was one of God's chosen people, the Israelites. The nation had not been faithful to God so He allowed the Midianites to rule over them for the last seven years. The Israelites had cried out to God because things were so bad. Gideon was at his family's winery, using the wine press to thresh some wheat (so the Midianites wouldn't find it), when an angel of God appeared. Read what happens in Judges 6:11-16.

How does the angel refer to Gideon? (v. 12)

How does Gideon describe himself? (v. 15)

What is God's reply? (v. 16)

Notice that God doesn't encourage Gideon in any way as to highlight Gideon's abilities. His response is to say, *I will be with you, therefore what I'm sending you to do WILL happen. End of story. Not you, ME.* What Gideon believes of himself is of no consequence. He will be a mighty warrior because God will see to it that he is.

Gideon isn't exactly convinced (still scared) and ends up requesting proof that God could come through in miraculous ways (v. 36-40). God passes Gideon's tests so he goes with the courage he has and rounds up an army of 32,000 men. Probably a reasonable amount since in 7:12 it says, *The Midianites, the Amalekites and all the other eastern peoples had settled in the valley, thick as locusts. Their camels could no more be counted than the sand on the seashore.* One version refers to them as *"a horde."* AKA: A frightening amount. That's when God tells Gideon to send some men home. He wants no mistake about who is saving them. He whittles it down to 300 men.

God knows he's still scared so he tells Gideon to sneak up close and listen to the enemy's conversation so he'll be encouraged. He does, he was, and what God had said happened. Gideon was a mighty warrior BECAUSE God was with him.

Based on what you know about David and Gideon, why do think David was not afraid going into his battle and Gideon was?

What did David know that Gideon didn't?

Because David had already had some hairy battles, he KNEW God was with him. Yes, he had some good skills with a slingshot, but we'd probably all agree when a razor-toothed, sharp-clawed beast of power and fury is charging you all bets are off. David was ultimately aware that without God he would have been bear buffet. Lion lunch.

David showed up in GOD'S power and he wasn't afraid.

Gideon isn't to be looked down upon either. He was just a guy who hadn't experienced God yet. He'd heard about the great things God had done in the past — for others — but he'd yet to understand what knowing God firsthand meant. While he started out scared, little by little God showed him He could be trusted and Gideon stuck with God, one step at a time. By all accounts, on the other side of the battle, Gideon became a David.

Step 1 **to move from fear to power is simply staying with God long enough to get there.** When we KNOW we can trust God, we'll start doing it. Below, jot any God-experiences you've had where you gained trust in Him. Then, on the *Trust Meter*, mark where you believe you're at with God currently.

|______________________|______________________|

A just starting Gideon — Full-on David

The next step is to make sure our thoughts aren't dragging us under. In our lives today, most of our battles are realistically fought internally. A war is going on inside us and that happens because we are used to operating out of how WE think and how WE feel. That's why we live defeated in some areas of our lives. That's why we don't have more joy or peace.

Step 2 **is to stop living as if what we feel is right and instead see what God says is true.** Our thoughts and feelings are often straight up LIES. Until we push back against current feelings, thoughts, and lies we will live in chaos and fear. We have to redirect our thinking. We have to check in with God.

Pastor Charles Stanley said, "*To renew your mind is to involve yourself in the process of allowing God to bring to the surface the lies you have mistakenly accepted and replace them with truth.*"

A tale as old as time is one of a down-and-outer living a hap-hazard life filled with tragedy and hardship. Then, low and behold, it's discovered that they are royalty. Once that is discovered, they move into the sprawling family estate where they live happily ever after.

It would be ridiculous to hear that they continued to live in squaller, struggling to eek out an existence once they knew who they really were. Yet, when we live in fear and captivity to wrong ideas, past hurts, nursing grudges and unforgiveness, battling chronic struggles, and living with endless worry instead of under God's protection, relying on Him to fight our battles, we are equally ridiculous. **Until you know who you are and start acting like it, nothing will change.** As we've discussed before, you will live out what you believe to be your reality.

Read 2 Timothy 1:7 in the margin. Sit with Jesus as you read that verse. What does Jesus want you to hear? Write it below.

For God has not given us a spirit of fear and timidity, but of power, love, and self-discipline. **2 Timothy 1:7 (NLT)**

Fear ends when we trust that God's got this. He is to be trusted to care for us and to lead us to a better place. We are to live by God's Spirit, by HIS power. We have everything we need to conquer all our fears, once we stop navigating life with former thoughts and feelings. We have to remember that we have the power to say no to wrong things now. We have the power to stop believing lies. We have the power to see and do things God's way.

Remember the Israelites who, when they got the "bad report" about the land God was sending them to, saw themselves as grasshoppers compared to the people who lived there? Joshua was one who brought a good report. His report was good because he looked through the lens of God's promises instead of with human eyes. Those who had given the bad report, who had no vision, perished in the wilderness. Joshua, in his trust of God, was given the privilege of finally leading God's people into the promised land. They still had to fight for the land, but they went with God's power, not their own, and they succeeded. God showed them that trusting Him was the way to move to the good life He had planned for them.

We have been given a spirit of power, love and self-discipline. What we may lack is time with God to learn how to trust Him and knowledge of who we are now and how God wants us to live. Those two things can be gained when we spend time reading God's word and hanging out with His Son. That's where fear ends and power begins.

Sit with Jesus. Talk to God

Read Joshua 1:1-9 and write down what stands out to you. Talk to Jesus about how YOU move from fear to power (v. 8 has some good insight).

Have I not commanded you? Be strong and courageous. Do not be afraid; do not be discouraged, for the LORD your God will be with you wherever you go. **Joshua 1:9**

Day 4

CONFRONTING IT ALL

A GOOD POINT

Victory can only be found on the other side of war.
-Jennene Eklund, author *Overthrow*

Depending on your current situation, you might be a little leary about what this day holds based on the title and the Good Point. The whole reason I knew this study is what God wanted me to write is because soooo many believers miss out on ALL that God has for them. Why? I believe it has to be one of two reasons. Either they just don't know things can be different or they are afraid of "going there" because it's not going to be pleasant. We have a tendency to pull back when things get uncomfortable. To avoid areas we don't want to be in. Areas of our lives that are downright painful. Where tears flow. Where great dread, unsettling worry, or fear live. Please hear me on this, it may not be pleasant, but on the other side is victory.

Get comfy with Jesus and tell Him what it would mean to have victory in those areas that you're struggling.

If we truly want to have a different life, our best life that God wants for us, the one where everything is as it should be, then we have to confront it all. As with all of your life from here on out, you will not be alone. The best way to dive into this study is to keep Jesus close and keep your victory in mind. We're also going to grab some pieces from our arsenal before we get into the thick of things. Look at Jesus and ask Him to calm any fears and to let you feel His closeness, comfort, and guidance today.

Let's prepare ourselves. Look up Ephesians 6:10-17. See yourself putting on each piece of armor as you read.

Where will your strength come from? (v. 10)

Now, read Psalm 55:16-18.

How will you come through your battle? (v. 18)

Flip back one page and read Joshua 1:9 in the margin.

How does God tell you to go into battle?

What does He say He will do?

Our battles may be hard, but we will win them, with God's help, and we will be victorious. Not only that, we will come through unharmed because God is with us. You CAN fight this battle no matter how hard.

Our goal today is to get on the road where we move away from lies we've believed for far too long, unload some dead weight that's dragging us down, and start putting our pasts behind us. Let's begin with an old story of a poor soul that many of us will be able to relate to.

> A man was trudging down the side of a road, bending under a heavy burden strapped to his back. When a kindly wagon driver came upon him he offered him a ride. The man happily accepted his offer, but when he climbed in he continued to bend under his load.
>
> "Why don't you lay down your burden?" asked the kindly driver.
>
> "Oh, I couldn't do that!" replied the man. "It's so much to ask you to help me out, I couldn't think of letting you carry my burden too."

That sounds crazy, but so many Christians live this way. We accept Jesus' salvation, but we don't let him help us with our burdens. In time, we'll feel like He's of no help at all, simply because we never let go of our baggage. So, if we ARE going to lay down our burden, first we have to grab onto it in order to hand it over. Doing that may cost us something.

1) Vulnerability and maybe some tears

I am not a crier, but when I went through the hardest season of my life I gave myself permission to be real. I cried. A lot. It was freeing. My son, who is a guy-guy — you know those guys who can remodel a house, fix their car, and bench press 350 lbs. — he feels no shame to cry. I love that about him. If something is hard or sad, life-changing or awe-worthy it's normal to cry. Give yourself permission. At least when you're alone with God.

2) Openness and Honesty

This is admitting to EVERYTHING and not ignoring or avoiding things you know are an issue for you. It's also being authentic about the depth and seriousness of your struggles. If it bothers you at all or eats at you it's a burden.

3) Admitting that you can't fix it

If you could have changed your thoughts, desires, or actions you probably would have by now. You have to admit you need help.

If any of that is bothering you right now can I give you a little advice? You put

Knowing Jesus Tip:
Whenever you come up against something in the Bible that you feel you can't line up with, know you are pushing back against, or don't want to own, get with Jesus about it. Talk to Him about why you are taking issue or offense with it, or feel you can't own it. Keep going after it with God until you get resolution and peace about it.

the armor on for a reason. Fight against those worries and say, *"NO! I WILL do all of those things because I WANT TO BE DIFFERENT!"* Remind yourself who you are (protected and loved by the God of the universe!), that you do not have to be afraid anymore because God said so, and He COMMANDS you to be strong and courageous (Joshua 1:9), that you will NOT listen to the evil one or your old self say you CAN'T anymore! Take a breath and with a warrior's spirit say, *"I'm doing this!"*

Are you with me?! We're going to work through some different areas you may need to confront. You and Jesus. What I am going to present is to get you thinking. You'll do the heavy lifting as you work through it sitting with Jesus. Is He with you? Are you with Him? If so, let's go.

In the first few weeks of our study, do you remember we had some scriptures where *strongholds* were mentioned? In 2 Samuel 22:2-3 David calls God his stronghold. A stronghold is a fortified place to protect us against attack. However, a stronghold of OUR making can be a very bad thing. In an attempt to protect ourselves, we can build up walls made up of things like lies, wrong beliefs, feelings, misunderstandings, distorted events, strong memories, assumptions, and skewed perspectives. What we've built up needs to come down. If we're living in our stronghold we can't be in God's.

To get started, read 2 Corinthians 10:3-5. We read part of this the first week.
Write down everything we are going to demolish.

It's time to take our thoughts captive so we can demolish everything that's holding us down and holding us back! Even if you feel like you aren't struggling with anything, you very likely have something you need to work on. Something God is going to bring to your mind as you go through these. Consider each one and hear what God is telling you. **Here are three key elements of negative strongholds and how we tear them down.**

1) Believing lies

How was sin first ushered into our world? Through a lie. The ancient serpent convinced Eve that eating the forbidden fruit would be a good thing for her. The way he got her to believe it was by using PART of the truth. Likely, if there are lies that you are believing, you believe them because they are SOMEWHAT true – therefore it's easy to believe it could ALL be true.

For example, if you believe that you will never have complete peace in your life and in your soul, that can feel true if you have NOT had peace for a very long time. It might feel true because when you tried different methods to gain peace they failed. Maybe there were many failed attempts. Maybe other people who are similar to you are in the same boat, compounding your idea that this is true. It may feel SO true that you think it IS true. In the NASB version, Proverbs 23:7 reads, *"for as he thinks within himself, so he is."* In other words, what you believe is how you'll live.

A good way to identify lies in your life is to answer a question. This isn't referring to what you'll *do* (like be in the Olympics or start your own business), but HOW you will BE. Fill in the blank with anything that comes to mind. Take your time and listen to what Jesus is directing you to.

I don't think I will ever ______________________________

How do we leave lies in the dust? Look up John 8:32 and write it below.

What sets you free?

What do you think lies do?

Start dissecting your lies with Jesus. Determine why they feel true. What part IS true? What is just true NOW? What part is not 100% or always true? Find Scripture that addresses your issues (see the tip in the margin). Jesus said the way to defeat lies is with truth. Go with Jesus and find some.

2) Pretending it's okay

First, there are some sinful things that we pretend are okay. Do we say we've forgiven someone, but secretly (or not so secretly) hold a grudge? Do we pretend that fantasizing about someone other than our spouse is okay? Do we gossip with our friends about someone else and write it off as what everyone does? Do we look at porn and think it's not really hurting anyone? Yet, there is a twinge, something inside you that tells you it's not okay. That would be the Holy Spirit. In John 16:8 Jesus says this about the Holy Spirit, *"And when he comes, he will prove the world to be in the wrong about sin..."* and verse 13 says, *"he will guide you into all the truth."* He knows you know it's wrong. Sit with Jesus and confess anything that's coming to mind.

What have you been pretending is okay?

There's another side of pretending. When people ask us how we're doing with something hard (after our marriage broke up, on the other side of rehab, when our kids never call, when our disease didn't get cured, or when we lost our job), we tell them we're doing fine. That is one thing. Knowing that's not true and telling OURSELVES it's okay, when we really don't think it is, is another. This is where that four letter word COPE comes into play.

It's the mentality that *things CAN'T get better so it is what it is. Suck it up.* This is NOT what God has planned for you. Look at 1 Thessalonians 5:23.

Knowing Jesus Tip:

If you want to find Bible verses on a particular subject, let's say *peace*, there are a couple of easy ways. First, if you have Internet access, in your search bar type, *"Scripture peace."* Starting searches with the word *Scripture* or *Bible* should ensure that what comes up are Bible verses. Also, many Bibles have a *concordance* in the back – an alphabetical list of common topics and where they are found in the Bible. There are larger, more complete Bible concordances sold separately as well. In your search, think of varying words and phrases that may be similar to search for.

The NLT version reads, *"Now may the God of peace make you holy in every way, and may your whole spirit and soul and body be kept blameless until our Lord Jesus Christ comes again."* In the verse, circle each area (the parts of you) that God says He is going to make perfect. Now underline the words that represents the *amount* of each of those areas He's going to perfect.

God is not a part-way God. He is an all-the-way, whole, completing God. Sit with Jesus and uncap what you've been coping with.

What have you just been pretending is okay?

How do we stop pretending? First, admit what the problem or concern is. Then take it to Jesus. Remember, in John 14:6 Jesus says, *"I am the way the truth, and the life."* Everything you want to get past, the WAY to a whole LIFE, is with Jesus. Don't stop working with Him until you are truly past it and at peace with it.

3) Keeping things in the dark

Not everyone is going to have something in this area. Don't feel like you need to go looking for something that isn't there. However, if you've been through something traumatic, life-altering, dealt with serious loss, or have an unsettling history keep going.

The Word gave life to everything that was created, and his life brought light to everyone. The [L]ight shines in the darkness, and the darkness can never extinguish it. **John 1:4-5 (NLT)**

Perhaps you dug out some dark stuff in the last section, if not, let's brighten things up. Read John 1:4-5 in the margin. The "Word" and the "Light" refer to Jesus. If you have darkness in your past, bringing Jesus (the Light) into that space also brings life. The darkness will not win.

How do we bring things to light? Be brave and take Jesus to your dark place and tell Him what you tell no one. What you try not to think about. You don't need to write it down. Just tell Him. Ask Him what to do and how to get past it. How to be free and walk in the light.

Sit with Jesus. Talk to God

Just telling Jesus your lies, pretendings, and darkness will make you feel lighter. Now, the key is continuing in the process. Keep the conversation going with Him every day until you are okay. Ask for God to guide you to people, resources, scripture, knowledge, and understanding in your situation. He will provide all you need. It will likely be a process. Remember, God knows how much time it will take for you to absorb, learn, and live fully in the light. Now that you're confronting it all, don't worry if it takes awhile to overcome some things, just expect to start moving forward and pay attention for God's leading. Smile. Peace, truth, and life are on the way.

Day 5
BE ENCOURAGED

A GOOD POINT

Never give up, for that is just the place and time that the tide will turn.
-Harriet Beecher Stowe

If you are reading this right now, I am so proud of you and so excited! We've been traveling together for six weeks now — you, me, and Jesus! I am realizing how much more I could tell you and I'm freaking out a little that I'm out of time! What I feel God wants to cover today is leaving you with a big batch of encouragement.

I know we've gotten into some deep waters along the way, but I pray you've also experienced some wonderful moments on the trail with Jesus. I pray that you've felt Him, heard His voice speaking just to you, sensed His presence, and are beginning to understand that KNOWING Him more and more will lead to everything you have never even thought you could have.

What I've learned on my journey with God is that it's never boring. You will have times where you feel like you're standing on the mountain tops with Him and other times like your trudging through a ravine. Some will fall in deep pits. It is all part of our journey here — one that God knows full well.

As we've discussed, no matter what you're going through, there IS a reason for it and things you will learn from both the lush pathways and the rocky roads. Things that will make you stronger, more reliant on God, kinder, gentler, more connected to God's plan and less connected to yours. There will be nothing wasted on your journey.

Perhaps the most important lesson I learned on my journey with God is the closer you stay to Him, and the better you know what He wants from you (what the Bible tells us), the better you will feel and the faster you will find yourself smiling at who you've become — and who you are yet to become.

As you continue to do life with Christ, there will be times you'll get discouraged. Maybe feel like you don't deserve to be happy. Feel like you are taking far too long to "get it." Think you'll never change. **Hear this: Discouragement and fear are NOT from God.** Nowhere in the Bible does it say that God's children should fear or worry. Instead, it all declares that God's true children are blessed and safe, that they should feel encouraged and joyful. Want some proof? Look up Romans 15:13.

What are you to be filled with?

What will you "overflow" with?

Perhaps we can feel discouraged because we think of all we'll give up by following Jesus. We have a skewed idea of what a life devoted to Him looks like. The world tells us we'll miss out. Let me tell you first hand: that is such a lie. I have never been more happy, filled with such joy and peace, and enjoying life like I have these last years of being all-in with Jesus. I know I will never be bored, even when I'm in my 80s. Life is extraordinary with Him! C.S. Lewis stated it perfectly –

> We are half-hearted creatures, fooling about with drink and sex and ambition when infinite joy is offered us, like an ignorant child who wants to go on making mud pies in a slum because he cannot imagine what is meant by the offer of a holiday at the sea. We are far too easily pleased.

When I was going through my hardest time, and I had some understanding of what God's Word said and how we should live, one of the things that stood out to me was that we were supposed to be joyful. See what Philippians 4:4 says.

What are we supposed to do always?

Now, look up John 16:33 and write the last two sentences below.

I like how the New King James Version puts it: *"...be of good cheer, I have overcome the world."*

...humbly accept the word planted in you, which can save you. Do not merely listen to the word, and so deceive yourselves. Do what it says.
James 1:21-22

Sometimes we can focus on all that we're *not* yet. How far we've *yet* to come, how much we *don't* know, how many *set backs* we've had. If you know that you are saved and that your true home is with Jesus in heaven, you should be joyful! Always! What's going on here can be hard and things take time, but God has a plan and that plan will work out. You do not need to wait to be joyful. Today is the day!

Take a look at James 1:21-22 in the margin.

We can't just read the Bible, we have to implement it or nothing changes. I wanted to do what God said about rejoicing so I told myself, *No more feeling discouraged! I will reset my default to joy! God says so!* I did and I was.

We have to stop allowing our wrong emotions to override what God declares. Push the reset everyday if you have to. Claim God's promises.

Another lesson I had to learn was that feeling miserable and discouraged, were NOT signs of humility, but a twisted form of pride. Feeling defeated and unhappy was realistically no more than saying, *"I am so specially flawed that what Jesus did was not enough."* I realized that when I focused on ME and my problems things were dark. When I focused on JESUS, on what's next, on God's promises, that He's here to help me, give me an abundant life, transform me, and use everything in my life for good, *I* was good. I knew I had no other choice than to start acting how one SHOULD act when everything is taken care of, now and forever. I became joyful.

Mark an X on the **Joy Meter** where you think your joy was when you started this journey six weeks ago and mark where it is now with a †. Talk to Jesus about why you marked it as you did.

|______________________________|______________________________|
Discouraged Joy-filled

Look back at the James verses again.
What is going to save you?

If you recall from our previous studies, Jesus is referred to as God's Word (John 1) *and* the Bible is God's Word. Jesus has saved your soul and now you need to *accept* (BELIEVE) that Word (Jesus and Scripture) and fill your mind, your time, and your life up with it. THAT is how you fulfill your life *here*. The WORD will save you from yourself, from the world, and from evil. Take it in daily and DO WHAT IT SAYS!

Sit with Jesus. Talk to God

Your life with Jesus will be something spectacular if you stay close to Him and drink in His Word and bask in the joy he offers. The Bible is a treasure trove of goodness, guiding, and grace that will lead you, shield you, and lift you. As we close today, read Jude 1:24-25 from the NLT version below. These verses have been game changers in my journey. I feel like they kind of sum up the whole Bible message for those of us who belong to Him. Sit for awhile with Jesus and process those words and today's lesson. Hear His words of encouragement.

Now all glory to God, who is able to keep you from falling away and will bring you with great joy into his glorious presence without a single fault. All glory to him who alone is God, our Savior through Jesus Christ our Lord. All glory, majesty, power, and authority are his before all time, and in the present, and beyond all time! Amen.

Do the wrap up at the end of your week — perhaps on your Day 6. It's a good way to recap what you've learned all week and capture the things that were most important to you.

Be Encouraged

WEEKLY WRAP UP

Write what point, quote, or Scripture stood out most to you this week

This week's memorization verse

Have I not commanded you? Be strong and courageous. Do not be afraid; do not be discouraged, for the LORD your God will be with you wherever you go. **Joshua 1:9**

Or, memorize the one that spoke loudest to you this week.

Hey! Here we are at the end of our journey! At least for now. I pray that your time on this leg of it has been meaningful. Honestly, I pray it's been life-altering. I pray it's given you some weapons and battle strategies to fight the good fight. To understand that we are in a war zone where the evil one is trying to take as many prisoners to hell with him as he can. To remember that as a child of God, you are saved, protected, and loved.

One of my favorite songs is Micah Tyler's *Different*. I cry every time I hear the line, ***I know that I am far from perfect, but through You the cross still says, "I'm worth it."*** Don't ever think you aren't part of God's plan. You are the whole reason there was a plan: God loved you and He didn't want to lose you.

In the song, Micah's request to be different pleads, *"So come take this beating in my heart and come and finish what you started. When they see me, let them see you."*

If you remember, we looked at Philippians 1:6 in Week 5 that says — *"being confident of this, that he who began a good work in you will carry it on to completion until the day of Christ Jesus."* You can be confident that what needs to be done in your life to make you complete is going to happen. Right now, when God looks at us, He sees Jesus — He sees perfection. What God will do IN you while you are here is to get you to believe you can be perfect. Little by little we start looking like Jesus because we learn we can be. You just have to keep traveling with Jesus, being mindful that you are following Him — not the other way around.

As you continue your journey to the life God has planned for you, the life YOU want for you, the thing that will trip you up the most is your daily decisions on who you are going to follow. The reality is, we are not in charge. Not following Jesus is choosing to follow Satan. We think we're "going our own way," but we're just going the way Satan wants.

When Eve chose to eat the fruit from the forbidden tree, she was choosing to listen to what the Devil had to say on the subject and reject what God had said. We don't like to think that we are aligning with Satan. We just want to have fun, get ahead in the world, say it like it is, and do what feels good. We just want to be happy. That's what Eve wanted too. It didn't work out like she thought and your attempts to do it your way won't either.

In the Bible, Eve was just the first of many who got it wrong and paid the price. God sent Jesus so we could have someone to copy, focus on, and to follow. Someone to show us the way to the life we REALLY want. The life where everything truly IS good. A life that is fulfilling, filled with peace, joy, and love.

People want to know what their purpose is. Read the tip in the margin.

Your purpose is to learn how to love. How to take your eyes off yourself and focus on the source of love (God) and to see the world as He does. To reach out in His love to those He puts in your path. The unique way you do that will be revealed to you as you continue to follow Him and get intentional in His Word. In that place, your burdens will ease. In time, you will leave them behind and they will not weigh you down in any way.

When you get to truly KNOW Him better, everything will make sense, and everything will change.

Know that I have been so blessed to be part of your journey! As we part company here is my prayer for you:

> *Father, I know how much you love this beloved child who has taken this journey with You. I pray that they continue seeking You intentionally and that they come to experience Your amazing grace, transformation, love, comfort, peace, and joy. I pray that they uncover the unique ways that you want to use them — the way that will bless them so richly. Father, let them continue to grow closer to You, to push through any adversity with You, learn to lean on You, and trust you with everything. May they come to richly know You better and better. In the mighty name of Jesus, Amen.*

Taking stock: Answer the questions below to process this week's study.

What were some key things that you felt Jesus nudging you about this week?

What was the most positive thing you felt Jesus wanted you to hear this week?

Sit with Jesus. Talk to God

Talk to Jesus about all you've learned in this study. This would be a good time to journal your thoughts and how you continue your journey following Him.

WHAT'S NEXT? 30 Day of Devotions!

On the following pages you'll find daily devotions that will help you continue to interact with God and stay in the Bible!

Knowing Jesus Tip:
Focus on living out the verses below well and everything will change.

The Greatest Commandment

"Teacher, which is the greatest commandment in the Law?"

Jesus replied: "'Love the Lord your God with all your heart and with all your soul and with all your mind.' This is the first and greatest commandment. And the second is like it: 'Love your neighbor as yourself.' All the Law and the Prophets hang on these two commandments."
Matthew 22:36-40

How to
CHOOSE A BIBLE

People are often confused when they go to purchase a Bible. There are a LOT to choose from and many versions. There are people way more qualified then me to give you all the details of why and how that happens, so, I'm going to keep it simple so you can get the basics and get started.

Why Bibles are different. When the people of God originally wrote what would be put into the Bible, the *Old Testament* was written primarily in Hebrew and the *New Testament* was mostly Greek. To give us a Bible in our language it had to be translated. If you are unfamiliar with other languages, not all words and thoughts can be translated word for word. For example, in Greek, there are many words for LOVE depending on the type of love (intimate love, brotherly love, family love, etc.). Therefore, utilizing a phrase may help the reader better understand. Different Biblical scholars approach those issues uniquely, so there are some variations.

Here are the main versions I use most myself and why.

NASB - New American Standard Bible. The NASB is touted by many biblical scholars as the closest word-for-word translation possible.

NIV - New International Bible (2011 update). *The NIV is the one we reference throughout this study unless noted otherwise.* The NIV is considered a close translation while also being broadly understood modern English. It has become one of the most popular and best selling modern translations so many people have this version already.

NLT - New Living Translation. This is the only Bible I used for many years when I was first learning and getting to know God. The NLT is what really made the Bible come alive for me. The scholars who worked on this made it their goal "to be both faithful to the ancient texts and eminently readable." Basically, they made it much easier to understand in the 21st century.

A word about King James - KJV. Many people grew up reading the *King James Bible* and I don't want to discount this version. If this is what you want to use, go for it! Many find it hard to understand as it is written in Old English and most of us just don't talk like that anymore. There is a *New King James* **NKJV** that has modernized the text which I do like much better.

Picking the right one. You should get ***The Holy Bible*** with both the *Old* and *New Testaments* included. Some will state they are *Study Bibles*. This just means there are some helpful notes to explain difficult passages or give you insight into the culture, geography, and other details. Not a bad idea. My NLT is a life-application study Bible. Most of my Bibles are also "Red Letter" Bibles because they have everything Jesus said in red ink. That helps to know when He's speaking.

You can get a free Bible with EVERY version.
I love having a printed Bible and I have a few I use almost daily. I also use a digital Bible because it makes it easy to switch between different translations super fast — and it's FREE. There are a few apps for free Bibles out there but I have always used YouVersion. To download your free Bible just go to **www.YouVersion.com**.

KNOWING BETTER

DAILY DEVOTIONS

As you continue hanging out with Jesus each day, this is what it should be like – you sitting as a child with your Father letting Him show you His world and teach you what you'll need to survive and thrive. We all start out our faith journey just taking everything in. It's a new life and we need to learn how to walk, talk, and eat solid food. As we grow, we'll question things, maybe a lot of things. As we gain understanding, learn how to trust well, and how to walk in step with Jesus, we'll gain clarity and confidence.

No matter how long we're here, we'll never outgrow our need to be close to our Savior. We all have more to learn. Jesus is leading us home, so don't let go of Him until you get there. Stay close by taking time daily to sit and talk with Him.

For the next 30 days, we'll give you a topic to think through and verses to look up and talk to Jesus about. The same holds true – see Him, tell Him everything, and position yourself to hear what He has to teach you. Knowing Him better, day by day, will take you to places you won't want to miss. Enjoy your time and your journey together.

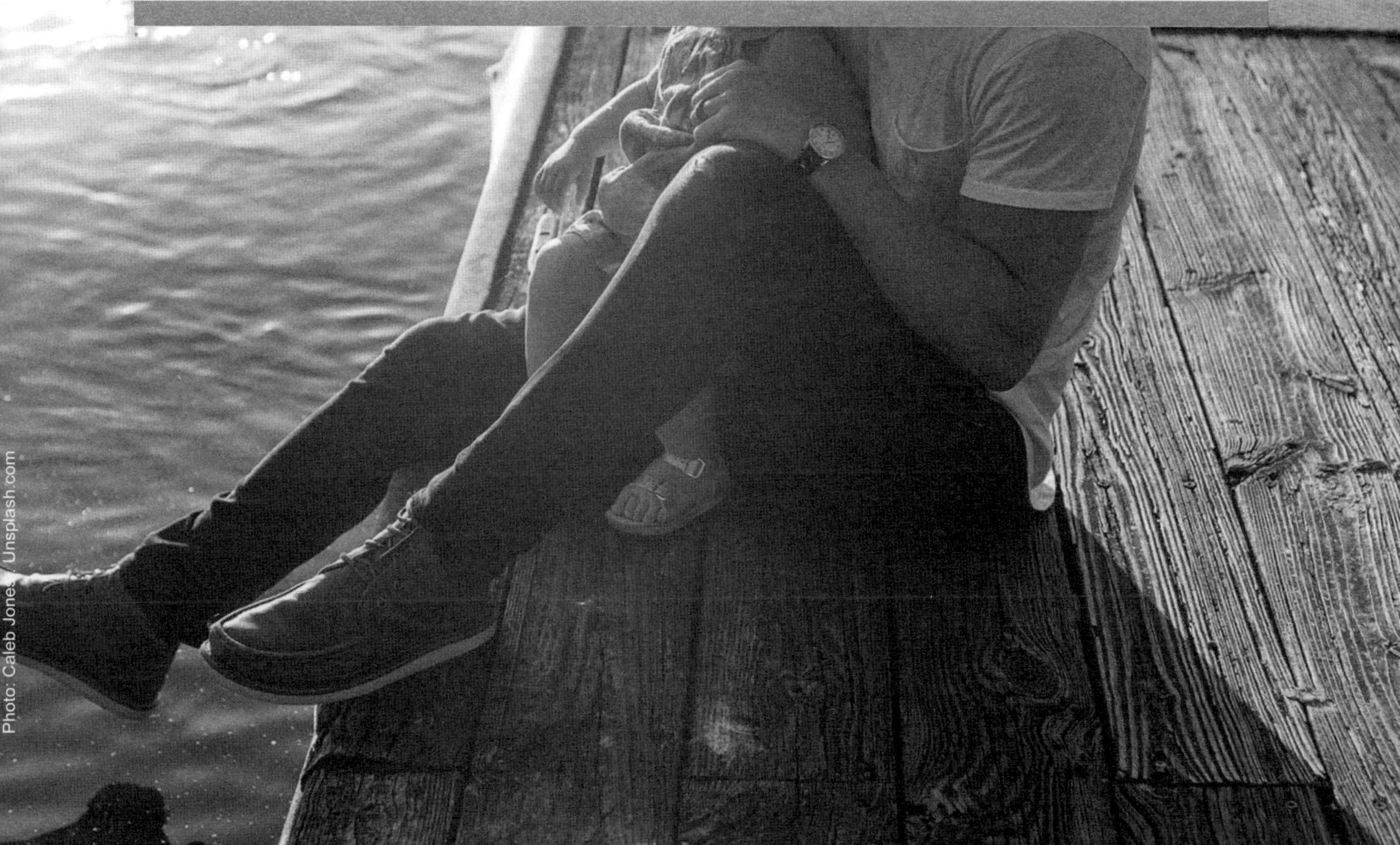

Photo: Caleb Jones / Unsplash.com

Day 1

FOCUS

Have intimacy with Jesus

"Now this is eternal life: that they know you, the only true God, and Jesus Christ, whom you have sent." *John 17:3*

What does it mean to be intimate with someone? We often equate intimacy with sex, but it actually refers to a deep familiarity or friendship with someone. Pastor Robert Morris defines it well:

Intimacy = Into Me See

It's letting someone in to know and understand who we really are. We allow them to see the real us: baggage, bruises, and bondage, as well as dreams, plans, and triumphs. In order to have a close, real relationship with anyone we have to be intimate with them. These deep relationships aren't ones you have with just anybody. They are special and intentional. The first one you need to nurture is the one with Jesus.

While Jesus had 12 disciples, as you read the Bible, you'll see there are times when He invites just three of them. Peter, James, and John were Jesus' closest friends and they got to experience things that the others only heard about later. Sometimes much later, as He asked them not to tell some events until an appointed time in the future. Probably the most amazing event they experienced was seeing Jesus change before their eyes, the Holy Spirit descending upon Him, and hearing the voice of God praise Him (Matthew 17:1-8).

Being a disciple of Jesus certainly lets us in on many great things, but who wouldn't want to be part of ALL that Jesus is doing and offering? Being intimate is a real commitment to being vulnerable and available to Jesus. You have to show up and reveal the real you — to talk about absolutely everything and to leave no stone unturned. You have to be willing to hear things about yourself — good and bad. Only in the deep KNOWING of Jesus, and allowing Him to know you, will you be fully satisfied in your life and in yourself.

As you choose to sit with Jesus each day, invite Him in and let Him really SEE you. As you grow in intimacy you become one with Him — transformed and fully connected to God.

Sit with Jesus and look up the scriptures. Note what stands out to you and write what you hear Him telling you.
Remember to note things about Jesus' character (who He is) and what He wants you to understand and do.

Psalm 63:1-11 • Luke 10:38-41 • John 15:1-11; 17:20-26

Talk to God.
Pray about what Jesus invited you into today.

Day 2

FOCUS

Be a doer

"These people come near to me with their mouth and honor me with their lips, but their hearts are far from me."
Isaiah 29:13

There was a man who had two sons. He told them both to go work in the family vineyard. The first son said no, but later, he changed his mind and went as his father had asked. The second son told his father he *would* go to work, but never did. Which son did what the father wanted?

This is the question Jesus posed to a group of religious leaders in Matthew 21:28-32. They replied that the first son had done what the father wanted. After all, it isn't what we *say*, but what we *do* that matters. Jesus agreed and proclaimed that the religious elite were NOT representatives of the first son, but were like the son who said the right things, but didn't DO the right things. We enjoy it when people get called out for their bad behavior don't we? Now, what about us? Do WE do what God wants or do we just give lip service?

The Bible is our handbook on how to do life. It tells us what to do, how to act, and what to avoid. It's not okay for us to claim to follow Christ, but then fail to do what He asks. We are called to love and forgive others, to allow God to change us, to serve, to put God first, to be humble, patient, and kind. Many things are for our own good — not to fear, to be courageous, to take our thoughts captive, not to worry. Yet we continue to allow these things in our lives. Jesus says when we do as He commands we show our love for Him. We don't need to try harder or do more, we simply need to draw closer to Jesus and ask Him to help us be doers and not be pretenders or avoiders. When we fall in love with Him, being doers will be something we WANT to do. The benefit of obeying Christ is a life filled with peace, satisfaction, and feeling refreshed and rebuilt.

Sit with Jesus and look up the scriptures. Note what stands out to you and write what you hear Him telling you.
Remember to note things about Jesus' character (who He is) and what He wants you to understand and do.

Luke 6:46-49 • James 1:22-25; 2:14-18 • John 14:15-24 • Isaiah 58:9-12

Talk to God.
Pray about what Jesus wants you to do today.

Day 3

FOCUS

Walk in the light

"Therefore, if anyone is in Christ, the new creation has come: The old has gone, the new is here!" 2 Corinthians 5:17

In the years I walked through the hardest season of my life, there came a point when I knew a lot of truth. I would recite my arsenal of scriptures over and over. I knew I was not supposed to be afraid. I knew I was supposed to be courageous and trust God. I knew that God said He would never leave me or forsake me. I knew the words said I was forgiven, eternally saved, and greatly loved. I knew, but I was still letting the past and the lies rule me.

I can't really tell you if this was a vision or a dream I had, but either way I saw myself in a room that was filled with light. The walls had windows all the way around. There were other people in the room, but I didn't look at them. We were all focused on ourselves, on our own problems. I was sitting in a chair and on my lap was a black rope. As I looked at it I heard a voice, which I knew was Jesus, say, *"You are free. You CAN leave this place and live like you are free...or are you going to tie yourself up again?"*

That's what happens when we know what God says, yet continue to be defined by our pasts, our struggles, and the *what-ifs*. Those lies and things that used to keep us captive are not binding us as much as we think they are. Jesus says we are a new creation. We have to focus on who we are now, who we are becoming, and WHO we are lead by now. Until we delight in God's promises and drink in all their goodness, we'll continue to be held hostage, be miserable, and ineffective. Our lives will be so much more when we press forward and focus on the road ahead. Push off the ropes of bondage and walk in The Light (with Jesus) from here on out.

Sit with Jesus and look up the scriptures. Note what stands out to you and write what you hear Him telling you.
Remember to note things about Jesus' character (who He is) and what He wants you to understand and do.

Psalm 1:1-6 • Philippians 3:9-14 • John 1:5 • Hebrews 10:23 • 1 John 1:9

Talk to God.
Pray about what Jesus wants you to walk in today.

Day 4

FOCUS

Keep the faith

"For we live by faith, not by sight." 2 Corinthians 5:7

Imagine you were one of Jesus' disciples. Day after day, you'd see him heal the sick. A disfigured hand would transform from shriveled to strong and normal, the paralyzed would walk, leprosy sores would disappear to reveal healthy skin, clouded eyes would clear and open wide at seeing shapes and colors, the deaf would become ecstatic as voices and music came to life. You'd watch Him turn water into wine and a child's lunch would multiply to feed thousands – with baskets of leftovers to take home. Then, one day, you're on a boat with Him and a storm comes up. Though it's a bad one, Jesus is sleeping through it. You yell to wake Him, thinking you're going under at any moment! Jesus awakes, gets up, and calms the storm. Of course He does. Afterward, you feel foolish for not trusting Him…especially since He remarked at how little faith you had in Him.

When life is good, it's easy to have faith. Or, rather, it's easy to *think* we have faith. Even though we've seen and heard of Jesus' miracles, we tend to forget about those when things get hairy. Of course Jesus can take care of any storm that comes our way, but until that idea is our default setting we won't have peace. Can we learn to have faith and stay calm no matter how much the winds kick up and the waves toss our ship at times?

Much of our trust in Christ simply has to come from our definitive owning of it. Initially, we may not feel we can trust, but we need to remind ourselves that Jesus IS our Saviour – even in the storms of life. Additionally, we must tell ourselves that having any feeling other than trust absolutely won't do. Jesus will either calm the storm or teach us how to focus on Him in the midst of it.

At first, we may lose our nerve and think we're going under, and it's okay to cry out to Jesus to save us. What we'll realize is that we only sink when we take our eyes off of Him. As we keep focus, we'll learn to trust automatically. As our faith grows, so will our confidence – not only in weathering storms, but in all that this life brings.

Sit with Jesus and look up the scriptures. Note what stands out to you and write what you hear Him telling you.
Remember to note things about Jesus' character (who He is) and what He wants you to understand and do.

Proverbs 3:5-6 • Matthew 8:23-27 • Matthew 14:25-33 • Colossians 3:2

Talk to God.
Pray about what Jesus wants you to have faith in today.

Day 5

FOCUS

Give a little grace

"Be merciful, just as your Father is merciful." Luke 6:36

We know we do it. We judge others on what they do and on what they don't do. Yet, when we view our lives, we give ourselves credit even when we just THINK about doing something good, plus we cut ourselves a LOT of slack for our wrongs. C.S. Lewis once said,

> "There is someone I love, even though I don't approve of what he does. There is someone I accept, though some of his thoughts and actions revolt me. There is someone I forgive, though he hurts the people I love the most. That person is me."

The Bible says that we ALL fall short of the glory of God. It says that NONE of us are good…not one. So why can we be so skimpy showing others grace or forgiving them when *they* mess up? WE certainly expect people to forgive us when we need a do-over, a second chance. Sometimes, when we start living like Jesus we can actually get worse! We see that others are not doing what Jesus says, and if *we* are, we climb up on our high horses and look down our noses at them. We start telling them what they need to do and how to act better. That's not our job.

Our job is to hang with Jesus and let Him change us. Our job is to tell others that Jesus loves them and that He can change their lives. Our job is to be hope givers, to be encouragers that it's not too late. Our job is to love others like we love ourselves, point people to Jesus, and let God do the rest.

Sit with Jesus and look up the scriptures. Note what stands out to you and write what you hear Him telling you.
Remember to note things about Jesus' character (who He is) and what He wants you to understand and do.

Matthew 6:14-15; 7:1-5, 12 • Ephesians 4:32 • 1 Peter 3:8-12

Talk to God.
Pray about who Jesus wants you to show grace to today.

Day 6

FOCUS

Stake your claim

"Praise be to the God and Father of our Lord Jesus Christ, who has blessed us in the heavenly realms with every spiritual blessing in Christ." Ephesians 1:3

My brother is a year older than me and while we would never admit it, we were basically best friends growing up. For some reason, when my sibling's friends were around, my brother felt it was his duty to tease me as much as humanly possible. He told me I was pretty. *Pretty ugly!* When the movie Dumbo was out he started announcing that my ears were about as big. (I didn't really get that one as my ears are more on the small side of normal.) The cherry on top was when he nicknamed me: *Doggifer.* That one lasted for years.

Who are we really? Are we who our family says we are? Are we who our friends believe us to be? Are we who society has labeled us? Despite what anyone calls us, good or bad, the only thing that matters is what our Heavenly Father says about us. Thomas Paine once said, *"Reputation is what men and women think of us; character is what God and angels know of us."* But it's even more than that.

God sees what we TRULY ARE even though we can't see it or even fully believe it right now. We may have a tarnished or unimpressive reputation, but God sees us with eyes that know how we'll turn out. He knows our eternal character is just like His Son's: Perfect.

As we truly believe what God says about us, we will live that way. We must own His assessment of us as a reality **(redeemed, friend of God, His child, a conquerer, chosen, holy)**. Not for our future-selves, but to start now, being all God sees us to be. You are made righteous by your faith in Jesus Christ, but it takes some time for you to start believing it and operating out of your true identity. Today, state out loud all the things God says you are and begin to stake your claim to those truths.

Sit with Jesus and look up the scriptures. Note what stands out to you and write what you hear Him telling you.
Remember to note things about Jesus' character (who He is) and what He wants you to understand and do.

Isaiah 43:1 • John 15:15 • Romans 8:16, 31-37 • 1 Peter 2:9

Talk to God.
Pray about who Jesus says you are today.

Day 7

FOCUS

Start bragging

"May I never boast except in the cross of our Lord Jesus Christ, through which the world has been crucified to me, and I to the world." Galatians 6:14

It's not hard for us to be braggers. We use all sorts of methods to impress people with who we are and what we've done. We can boast about success, material possessions, our attractive or smart spouse, our popular kid, and how we help the homeless. We can even do a shock and awe brag about how many times we've been married, hospitalized, or jailed. Bragging comes when we feel that we have something above and beyond others.

There are several verses in the Bible that tell us we should never brag. Basically, because bragging is all about YOU. Since we are supposed to be dead to ourselves and alive in Christ (Galatians 2:20), the Apostle Paul reminds us that we should only brag about Jesus and what He's done. So, to do that, think about what you would say about yourself if you couldn't include what you do for a living, what your marital status is, how many kids you have, what you're going to college for, or what you've done in life. What would you say about who you are without mentioning anything you have or do?

Yesterday's devotions may give you a start. Today, add to your list of all that God says you are by looking up the verses below and writing *"I am"* statements. You should be able to come up with at least a dozen. A couple you may find are, *"I am rescued,"* and *"I am eternal."* Avoid saying, *"I CAN have peace."* Realize you just need to start owning it: "I am at peace!"

This is the only way to boast — in all that God has provided to you. Brag away and find your true self!

Sit with Jesus and look up the scriptures. Note what stands out to you and write what you hear Him telling you.
Remember to note things about Jesus' character (who He is) and what He wants you to understand and do.

Isaiah 41:9-10 • Colossians 1:13-14 • 1 John 5:11-14, 18 • Galatians 6:14 • Philippians 4:6-7

Talk to God.
Pray about all that Jesus wants you to boast about today.

Day 8

FOCUS

Feed yourself well

"Taste and see that the Lord is good;" Psalm 34:8

In the 1960s, the average weight of an American woman was 140 lbs. and men were a lean 166. Forty years later, after the dawn of microwavable meals, ready-to-eat treats, and drive-thru restaurants women tip the scales at an average of 170 lbs. and men weigh in at just shy of 200. When we have the ability to feed ourselves quickly, easily, and deliciously, apparently we do it.

We also have access to a lot of other delights we can feast on. We can feed ourselves from an endless buffet of entertainment, self-gratification, relationship connections, knowledge, and education. Just like eating all we have available to us leads to health problems and a shape we don't want, consuming all that the world offers can leave us feeling miserable and unhealthy in our soul.

Jesus meets such a woman at a well. She is a woman who has had five husbands and the man she is living with currently is not her husband. She's alone at the well to get water, during the hottest part of the day, because she's avoiding the other women who don't want anything to do with her. Jesus tells her that if she drinks the water He offers she would never be thirsty again. She thinks that sounds pretty good.

Jesus wants us to know that all the things we take into our body are simply an attempt to quench something in our lives – yet none of it lasts. We have to keep going back to drink because nothing ever satisfies us for any length of time. Jesus tells us if we would fill ourselves with all that He is and what He offers, we would find the fulfillment we are looking for.

What are you feeding yourself? Are you consuming things that leave you feeling bad, sick, disgusted, unfulfilled? Jesus wants us to try things His way. When we start eliminating the bad and replace it with what moves us toward Christ, we will find how much less we need from the world. Taste and see that the Lord is good and you'll leave life's table satisfied.

Sit with Jesus and look up the scriptures. Note what stands out to you and write what you hear Him telling you.
Remember to note things about Jesus' character (who He is) and what He wants you to understand and do.

John 4:1-42 • Matthew 4:4 • 1 Peter 2:1-3

Talk to God.
Pray about what Jesus wants you to feed on today.

Day 9

FOCUS

Let Jesus counsel you

"And he shall be called Wonderful Counselor, Mighty God, Everlasting Father, Prince of Peace." Isaiah 9:6

One of the names Jesus has is *Wonderful Counselor*. I hadn't really thought about what that meant before, but when I heard it again around Christmastime it dawned on me how true that is about Him. I often tell people Jesus is the best counselor you will ever have. If you've never been to one before, here's how it typically works: You sit down in a comfy place and you tell the counselor your issues — your problems. They listen and then they ask you questions. Questions that make you think about your situation in ways that you hadn't considered. Sometimes in ways that you don't like. Questions that get to the TRUE issue and the BEST solution. Eventually, you end up hearing an answer to your problem and it comes out of your own mouth. It's a process to get you to see something your weren't able or willing to see before.

The word *wonderful* that appears in the Isaiah verse actually means *incomprehensible*. Jesus is a counselor that will wow you. When you sit with Jesus each day and pour out your life to Him, He counsels you, guides you, and gives you wisdom and insight. Jesus is patient and a great listener — especially since He can hear even what we're not saying. Since He is also Mighty God, He has all the guidance we will ever need to help us when we come to Him. Don't miss out on all the hidden treasures waiting for you. Let Jesus counsel you each day.

Sit with Jesus and look up the scriptures. Note what stands out to you and write what you hear Him telling you.
Remember to note things about Jesus' character (who He is) and what He wants you to understand and do.

Psalm 139:1-6 • Proverbs 3:5-6 • Colossians 2:2-3 • Hebrews 4:14-16

Talk to God.
Pray about what you need Jesus to give you counsel on today.

Day 10

FOCUS

Stay in the story

"To those who listen to my teaching, more understanding will be given. But for those who are not listening, even what little understanding they have will be taken away from them." Mark 4:25 NLT

Back in the '80s there was a movie titled, *The NeverEnding Story*. It was about a land filled with interesting and varied characters that thrived or died depending on one thing: The belief of the reader that the storybook character's lives were happening for real — and in real time. If the reader didn't believe and participate in their story, the inhabitants and their world would disappear. If the reader *did* get involved in the story, thereby proving his or her belief, the storybook citizens and their lives would be restored and their story would continue. The Bible and you have a similar existence.

The difference is, if you fail to continue in the never-ending story of God, you and your world will disappear. If we are not actively involved in the journey with Jesus, we will forget what's real and any goodness and truth we experienced will cease to exist for us. Over time, our hearts will be hardened and we will no longer understand what we used to know. We must make sure we are engaged in the reality of what Jesus is doing in His story. This keeps us alive and well. If we stop participating, our lives will not thrive — they will slip away.

Don't let your story stop progressing. Stay active in Christ's Book and be restored, renewed, and alive.

Sit with Jesus and look up the scriptures. Note what stands out to you and write what you hear Him telling you.
Remember to note things about Jesus' character (who He is) and what He wants you to understand and do.

Proverbs 28:9 • Matthew 25:14-30 • John 15:8-11 • Hebrews 4:16, 11:6

Talk to God.
Pray about how Jesus' story involves you today.

Day 11

FOCUS

Look outward

"No one should seek their own good, but the good of others." 1 Corinthians 10:24

It's not hard to focus on yourself. You are with yourself all day, everyday. When you look in the mirror, there you are. You have to wash yourself, move yourself out of the sun or the cold, and do something meaningful to contribute to the world. You naturally have to take care of yourself, but what if, just for once, you didn't think about yourself beyond absolute necessities? What if you took all the energy you typically expended on yourself — thinking about what you might buy to make yourself look or feel better, worrying about something, dwelling on your feelings, or replaying that event in your mind where you are in the starring role...whether good or bad — and instead, thought about someone else?

Since the Bible tells us to love others as ourselves, then what would happen if we took today and did that? Might you pray for another person who is going through something hard? You might find yourself making time for a phone call to a co-worker, friend, or sibling. You might pay for the guy's coffee behind you in the drive-thru. You might be nicer to your boss. You might research what the homeless shelter needs....and then rally friends to donate it. You might say, "Hi!" to your neighbor, help someone reach the high shelf in the grocery story, and remember the couple at church who just took in four foster kids. You might find a non-profit is looking for some helpers for a weekend or are in need of someone with your skills on their board. You may even find that your brother's new business venture is really interesting — and saying so would mean the world to him. One thing you will find is that thinking about others and taking actual steps to help them and show love to them will make you feel better about yourself.

When you do what God says, and focus outside of yourself, you will find your life works better. Plus, you'll feel God's love in your life. You'll realize that looking outside of yourself accomplishes more than you imagined. Take today and reroute every thought about yourself to someone else and see what happens.

Sit with Jesus and look up the scriptures. Note what stands out to you and write what you hear Him telling you.
Remember to note things about Jesus' character (who He is) and what He wants you to understand and do.

Matthew 6:31-33 • Romans 12:10 • Philippians 2:4 • 1 John 4:7-8 • 1 Timothy 5:8

Talk to God.
Pray about who Jesus wants you to focus on today.

Day 12

FOCUS

Learn from the best

"Those who trust in themselves are fools, but those who walk in wisdom are kept safe." Proverbs 28:26

My four-year-old granddaughter stayed with us last weekend and she drew a picture of our family. Based on her example, I want you to draw a picture of yourself in the space above. First, draw a circle about the size of a quarter. Inside the circle make two dots for eyes and draw a smile. Now, draw two lines a couple of inches long coming from the bottom of the circle — they don't have to be even. How do you look?

If you ask another four-year-old what's wrong with it, they might instruct you to add arms. Better draw some on…to the sides of your head. Not much of an improvement is it?

When we see these immature drawings we think they're cute, but we don't think they are good, or accurate. I saw a news story years ago about an art teacher who got tired of seeing these types of drawings. As she sat with a group of kindergarteners she explained what they were missing and showed them how to adjust their approach. They were able to understand and the next sketches were dramatically better. They just needed to be taught by someone who knew how to do it — the right way.

Too often in this life, we simply do what we think is best or take advice from equally unskilled or uninformed people. The Bible tells us that blind people being led by blind people isn't going to go somewhere good. If we want to do art better, we should listen to an artist. If we need help learning to budget our money, we should listen to a financial planner. If we want to know how to do life, we need to get advice from The Creator of life. Listen to Jesus and you'll soon understand how to draw a beautiful life.

Sit with Jesus and look up the scriptures. Note what stands out to you and write what you hear Him telling you.
Remember to note things about Jesus' character (who He is) and what He wants you to understand and do.

Proverbs 3:5-6, 12:15 • Matthew 15:14 • Philippians 4:9 • 2 Timothy 2:15, 3:16

Talk to God.
Pray about what Jesus wants you to learn from Him today.

Day 13

FOCUS

Give up your hard edges

"Jesus replied, "Anyone who loves me will obey my teaching. My Father will love them, and we will come to them and make our home with them." John 14:23

A friend had a son who was struggling with a serious issue. She asked me what the Bible said about it and I pointed her to several scriptures on the topic. When she read them she was very disturbed because the verses didn't line up with how her son was living. In her mind, she saw her son as a square peg and God's plan as a round hole — her son was never going to fit into the plan.

Her solution was to get a second opinion. When their advice was the same, she asked another, and another. Eventually she found a voice that said what she wanted to hear. She didn't want the truth, she wanted someone to say it wasn't a problem. The Bible doesn't tell us that God will conform to our lifestyle or our way of thinking. God isn't here to do what WE want. He knows what's best and He won't let us be anything less. The good news is, God can do what we can't do on our own: change us.

We all, ALL, have to allow God to change us. We may look at others and see what needs to be altered, but so often we forget to look at ourselves first. Things like pride, putting other people and things before God, and gossiping can weigh us down greatly, but we don't even think about those because so many people do the same.

The Bible tells us that we are ALL square pegs and NONE of us fit as we are, but God has a way to round off our edges and to transform us so that we DO fit into His plan. When we hang out with Jesus everyday and read the Bible, we will understand what to do and how to live. When we stop fighting against what God says, being rigid and unwilling to accept change, we will be very uncomfortable. Likely, fear and worry will be our companions. When we read the Bible and make a decision to live out what the Bible says (relying on God's Holy Spirit to empower us), we will find that our hard edges soften and that change wasn't as impossible as we imagined.

Sit with Jesus and look up the scriptures. Note what stands out to you and write what you hear Him telling you.
Remember to note things about Jesus' character (who He is) and what He wants you to understand and do.

2 Timothy 4:3 • Matthew 7:3 • Romans 3:23-24 • Romans 2:13 • Romans 8:1-17

Talk to God.
Pray about what hard edges Jesus wants you to let Him work on today.

Day 14

FOCUS

Stay close

"But as for me, it is good to be near God." Psalm 73:28

A friend who was a drug addict for many years found salvation in Christ and her life was redeemed. After a few years of being sober, she thought she was invincible and that her problems were behind her. She thought because she was saved that she was safe from the temptations of the world. Before she knew it, she was using again. When she went to prison she reconnected with Jesus and saw where she went wrong — it was her pride that drug her under.

She forgot that it was being close to Jesus that saved her, not her own willpower. When she'd gotten better her pride told her she was good to go. She stopped reading the Bible as much. Stopped talking to Jesus as often. Thought she'd be okay to be with old friends. Have just one drink. She paid the price.

Today, she has been clean and sober for seven years and she stays very close to Jesus. She is so incredibly humble, crediting EVERYTHING good in her life to God's mercy and grace. Whenever anyone compliments her on her success and how she has helped so many people fighting the same battles, she simply smiles and exclaims, "Team Jesus!" She knows she will only be safe from the world by staying close to her Savior.

I too, have seen many start out strong only to falter. Doing jail ministry, I see those who show up for Bible Study, have lots of questions, and genuinely seem to be following Jesus. It's easy to be all-in when you don't have a lot of other options or life is hard and you need answers. Yet, when inmates get out, or things are going well again, their interest goes to other things and they leave Jesus and the pursuit of a different life. This is just as true for those on the outside who are sitting in church every Sunday.

When you set out on a journey with Jesus, commit to stay close EVERY day. Don't let your pride or lies (like you don't need Jesus as much) pull you off the path.

Sit with Jesus and look up the scriptures. Note what stands out to you and write what you hear Him telling you.
Remember to note things about Jesus' character (who He is) and what He wants you to understand and do.

Ephesians 2:8-9, 4:1-3 • Romans 12:3 • 1 John 3:7 • Revelation 2:4

Talk to God.
Pray about what Jesus is cautioning you about today.

Day 15

FOCUS

Check yourself

"Whatever happens, conduct yourselves in a manner worthy of the gospel of Christ." Philippians 1:27

Has anyone ever said something about you and your response was maybe like, *"Well, that's just how I am."* I was in a group of women once and one gal used a lot of cuss words. Another woman called her out on it and she said, *"I always swear. That's just me."* A woman told me about a close friend of hers who was a pastor. They would often get together and talk about *"God stuff"* while they had several drinks. The pastor had always been a big drinker — *that's just how it was.* A family reported that their father, who'd gone to church his whole life, was typically a great guy. Yet, when something annoyed him he became abrupt and even rude or hurtful to people. That's what he'd grown up with and voiced, *"That's just my personality!"*

At some point, we have to check ourselves and remember that we are supposed to be a new creation (2 Corinthians 5:17), but even more than that, we have to ask ourselves a question. *"If Jesus DIED to save me – from death and suffering in a horrible place called Hell – is this how I should be acting? Is THIS what He gave up his life for? For me to behave in a way that doesn't honor that?"*

When we don't change our bad behavior and our sinful practices, we are truly disrespecting what God did for us. If you think that is okay, because He is a forgiving God, you need to spend some serious time with Jesus. I doubt any of us would feel it would be just fine to cheat on our spouse or call them names just because they had forgiven us for those things before. It's time to check ourselves and start acting in a way that truly honors Jesus — and all those we profess to love.

Sit with Jesus and look up the scriptures. Note what stands out to you and write what you hear Him telling you.
Remember to note things about Jesus' character (who He is) and what He wants you to understand and do.

1 Corinthians 3:16, 10:31 • Ephesians 4:29-32 • 1 Peter 3:8-12 • Titus 1:7

Talk to God.
Pray about what Jesus is showing you today about ways you aren't honoring Him.

Day 16

FOCUS

Keep trying

"So do not fear, for I am with you; do not be dismayed, for I am your God. I will strengthen you and help you; I will uphold you with my righteous right hand." Isaiah 41:10

Matthew 14:22-33 is the well-known story about Jesus walking on the water. (If you aren't familiar with it, take a moment to read it.) They'd had a big day and Christ's disciples went out in the boat while He stayed back to pray. When He was done, it was nighttime so He took a stroll across the water to meet up with them. Since none of them had ever even considered that anyone could walk on the water (due to those things called gravity and buoyancy) they freaked out. Once they realized it was Jesus, Peter got pumped and asked if he could try that. Jesus said sure.

Peter did get out of the boat, but as he began walking toward Jesus he got scared and started to sink. He yelled to Jesus to save him. Often people use this passage to point out that we need to keep our eyes on Jesus when things get hairy. So true. However, there is something else very important to notice.

How many of the disciples even TRIED to walk on the water? Only Peter. That was remarkable for a couple of reasons. One, it showed amazing trust in Jesus. Plus, Peter wasn't getting out onto a calm, glassy surface. It talks about the wind "buffeting the waves." Many of us are okay following Jesus when things are calm, but as soon as things get a little stormy we're holding on tight where we're at.

Oh, and by the way, PETER DID walk on water… until he over-thought it and freaked himself out. BUT, even then he remembered that Jesus would save him. Sometimes we'll have to step out onto the waves, in the storm, but knowing that Jesus will save us should encourage us to try to follow His lead. We might sink, now and again, but we'll also feel Christ's hand pull us up when we do.

Who do you think learned more that day, experienced the unheard of, and had a great story to tell? The ones who stayed in the boat or the one who ventured out with Jesus? Jesus pointed out Peter's lack of faith when it got the better of him, but where was ANY faith among those on the boat? Even if you feel like you sink more than you walk in faith, continuing to TRY to follow Jesus' example will give you one whale of a tale.

Sit with Jesus and look up the scriptures. Note what stands out to you and write what you hear Him telling you.
Remember to note things about Jesus' character (who He is) and what He wants you to understand and do.

Isaiah 26:3 • Psalm 37:4-6 • Proverbs 24:16 • Zephaniah 3:17 • Matthew 19:26

Talk to God.
Pray about how Jesus wants you to take a step in faith with Him today.

Day 17

FOCUS

Live wisely

"Yes, a person is a fool to store up earthly wealth but not have a rich relationship with God." Luke 12:21 NLT

A number of years ago, an Australian nurse who cared for people during the final weeks of their lives began asking them if they had any regrets in life. The top five did NOT include wishing they'd been more successful or wealthy. The biggie was not living the life THEY wanted, but what someone else expected. Another common regret was having worked too much and having missed out on life at home — real life.

In Luke 12, Jesus tells the story of a man who had it all and had it in abundance. When his crops produced a bounty he found he had nowhere left to store it all. He decided he'd tear down his barns, build bigger ones, and sit back and enjoy the good life. Jesus warns us, while that all sounds great, what the man didn't know was that he was going to die that very night. What the man had spent his whole life on was pointless. Somebody else would take over his wealth and property.

Jesus tells us the man was a fool to spend his life striving for something temporary while skipping over what would be eternal — a rich relationship with God. What are you spending most of your time striving for? What would become of it if you don't make it until tomorrow? What will become of YOU? If you knew time was up now, what would you wish you'd done differently?

Start living wisely today and prioritize your relationship with Jesus. Then, when it is your last day here you won't leave with any regrets.

Sit with Jesus and look up the scriptures. Note what stands out to you and write what you hear Him telling you.
Remember to note things about Jesus' character (who He is) and what He wants you to understand and do.

Luke 12:13-21 • Matthew 6:25-33 • Colossians 3:1-2 • 1 Peter 1:3-4

Talk to God.
Pray about how Jesus wants you to live today so you have no regrets in the future.

Day 18

FOCUS

YOU, be ready

"You also must be ready, because the Son of Man will come at an hour when you do not expect him." Luke 12:40

When a teacher saw that one student failed to hand in the homework assignment, she asked for an explanation. *"My friend made me go with her to the psychic on the way home from school yesterday. The psychic told me that if I did my homework I'd lose my leg! I didn't want that to happen so I didn't do it – and even if I had I wouldn't be able to walk so I couldn't hand it in anyhow!"*

Our excuses can be pretty strange and we often try to point the finger at others who are letting us down, holding us back, and withholding help. Jesus tells the story of ten bridesmaids who were waiting for the groom to arrive so they could go into the wedding party. They all came so they could be part of the party, but only half of them brought what was needed. When the groom was almost there, the ones who had not prepared scrambled to get what the groom would be expecting. They asked the ones who had come prepared if they could borrow what they needed from them. The wise bridesmaids said no – they only had enough for themselves. As the five left to get what they needed, the groom arrived, let the bridesmaids who were ready into the wedding party, and shut the doors. He did not go back to let the others in when they finally arrived.

Too often, we think we'll have time later to do the right thing, focus on Jesus, and be there when He's ready for us. Additionally, instead of taking time to be ready ourselves, we go to others who live for Jesus to see if we can glean some of what they have. Being prepared means knowing what the Bible says and doing those things. Getting yourself ready is growing in your faith and your knowledge – more than just relying on what your Sunday School teacher shares or taking notes from your pastor's sermon once a week. It's taking the initiative to mature in your faith and to be actively engaged in the process yourself. Jesus wants YOU to be ready at all times to serve Him, to go with Him without notice, and to take responsibility if you want to be included in the party at the end. Jesus is looking at YOU to be ready for Him at all times. Are you?

Sit with Jesus and look up the scriptures. Note what stands out to you and write what you hear Him telling you.
Remember to note things about Jesus' character (who He is) and what He wants you to understand and do.

Matthew 25:1-13 • Matthew 24:36-44

Talk to God.
Pray about what Jesus wants you to be prepared for today.

Day 19

FOCUS

Talk to Me

"Devote yourselves to prayer, being watchful and thankful." Colossians 4:2

You've probably seen those commercials asking for financial aid to help alleviate the suffering of starving children. The agencies do their best to show us the sad, sunken faces, and acquaint us with their dire circumstances and the realities of their poverty. How much different it would be if one of those children knocked on your front door. Your response would be quite different. Why? Because the idea of starvation would go from concept to reality.

We won't get excited about a cause or a person if we aren't in relationship with them. The same is true with your relationship with Jesus. You won't be excited about Him if He isn't a reality to you every day. Perhaps that's why the Apostle Paul tells us to, *"Pray without ceasing."* That just means you do it all the time. No matter what's going on, you should be talking to Jesus about it — getting His input, blessing, and help.

The Bible tells us to both pray on our own and to pray with other believers. First, we want to pray by ourselves. If you aren't spending time alone with someone you ARE NOT in a relationship with them. Even Jesus went off by Himself to have time to talk to His Father. This is where we can't fake it. If we don't want to spend time with Jesus there's probably something we don't want to discuss or we don't see it as a benefit. Believe me, talking to Jesus will result in what you really want for your life and the benefits will become obvious.

Next, get together with others and pray. Share what you're struggling with and pray for each other and for the common good. As you stay in communication with God, and in community with others, you'll be amazed at the wonderful results.

Sit with Jesus and look up the scriptures. Note what stands out to you and write what you hear Him telling you.
Remember to note things about Jesus' character (who He is) and what He wants you to understand and do.

1 Thessalonians 5:16-18 • Matthew 6:6 • Mark 1:35 • Luke 5:16 • Matthew 18:20 • James 5:16

Talk to God.
Pray about your prayer time with Jesus today.

Day 20

FOCUS

Listen to My Spirit

"We do not know what we ought to pray for, but the Spirit himself intercedes for us..." Romans 8:26

Sometimes it can be difficult to know what to pray for. If you are in a tense relationship with your spouse you may have a tangle of emotions. One minute you want it to be great like it was in the beginning and the next you're wishing they'd leave and never come back. It's hard to know what's right sometimes and what to pray for. You know what you WANT to pray for, but you also sense what you SHOULD pray for.

Even if we are doing life fairly well, because we know how much work WE need while we're in the process of becoming more like Jesus, we can find our prayers pretty self-centered. What are we even supposed to pray for?

First, the Bible tells us that the Holy Spirit is right there with us. HE is praying for us when we don't know what's what. When you feel confused or torn, simply ask God to help you pray for the right things. Tell Him you don't know what to pray for and that you need His help. Ask God to help you want and pursue the right things.

The Bible also says to, *"Pray in the Spirit"* all the time. The Holy Spirit is inside of you, so just shut yourself off and listen to Him. Ask Him what He wants you to pray for. People, projects, and problems will pop into your mind. You may think about a neighbor who is having a health crisis, be struggling with an issue at work, remember a friend who doesn't know Jesus, think about a Christian group who is making a difference, or feel concern about an upcoming election or leader. Spend some time talking about those thoughts with God. Ask for His guidance, intervention, comfort, revelation, protection, or blessing as you feel led. The more you pray "in the Spirit" regularly, the more you will find you'll know what to pray for.

Sit with Jesus and look up the scriptures. Note what stands out to you and write what you hear Him telling you.
Remember to note things about Jesus' character (who He is) and what He wants you to understand and do.

Ephesians 6:18 • Romans 8:26 • 1 Peter 5:7 • 1 Timothy 2:1-2

Talk to God.
Pray about what Jesus wants you to pray for today.

Day 21

FOCUS

Tell Me about it

"So if the Son sets you free, you will be free indeed." John 8:36

A little girl, about eight-years-old, went to her mother quite concerned. *"Mother, why am I so naughty?"* She knew her behavior wasn't right, but she couldn't seem to change it. *"I thought Christians were always good, but no matter how much I try I just can't help being naughty."* How many of us feel exactly the same way?

The girl's mother gave her the answer — and it will be your answer too, *"I expect that the reason is because you try to make yourself good. We can never make ourselves good, no matter how much we try. Only our Heavenly Father can make us good, and we must just trust Him to do it. Whenever you feel tempted to be naughty, if you will tell Him all about it, and ask Him to make you good, and then will trust Him to do it, He will be sure to take all your naughty away."* Her daughter tried this approach and it worked.

A few days later, the little girl burst out, *"Oh, mother, aren't you glad Heavenly Father is making me so good? He is going to make me a great deal gooder, but aren't you glad He has made me as good as He has this far?"* The advice came from a faithful mother who lived over 150 years ago. Her biggest revelation was realizing that this one piece of knowledge was something that very few people knew — how to live in freedom from sin in the here and now.

I can tell you it is possible because I experienced the same results. You can have total freedom from the things that weigh you down by telling Jesus about temptations and trials as soon as they appear, moment-by-moment, day-by-day. It seems to be a secret to many, but the Bible is clear that we can have this life of peace and joy — free from guilt, fear, worry, and sin-riddled lives. We just need to tell Jesus about it and discover that our naughty will leave. Oh, it will try to return often, but Jesus will take it each time we ask. He will make us good and we will know that He will make us a great deal gooder — one day at a time.

Sit with Jesus and look up the scriptures. Note what stands out to you and write what you hear Him telling you.
Remember to note things about Jesus' character (who He is) and what He wants you to understand and do.

Romans 6:6-7 • Galatians 5:1 • 2 Corinthians 5:17, 21 • 1 John 1:7 • Matthew 6:34

Talk to God.
Pray about what sins you need Jesus to take from you today.

Day 22

FOCUS

Keep it alive

"But grow in the grace and knowledge of our Lord and Savior Jesus Christ." 2 Peter 3:18

When I was a kid, our front porch had a nice wide railing around it. As we stepped into our make-believe world we'd tie on a baby blanket cape or grab the corners of it to create a parachute. We'd climb on top of the porch railing and leap from imagination into reality – sort of. For the four feet from railing to grass, our fantasy of flight worked. We knew what we had wasn't enough to REALLY let us fly. We just pretended like it would. We can wear our religion similarly.

I once heard a pastor give another analogy that I like. He compared most people's religion to a stick horse. A child gallops around the yard imagining that the horse is carrying her, yet the truth is, the child is carrying the horse. Many people get acquainted with religion and have some ideas of what it's supposed to do for them so they pretend like it's all good. We can make excuses or flat out lie about our faith and what we're getting out of it. Religion that WE carry is exhausting and discouraging. Pretending our faith is more than it is will leave us in a hard place when we are in real need. We'll see that our imaginary faith is not enough to really carry us, save us, or let us fly. We'll see it's just a fantasy. Make-believe.

We need to grow our faith and continue learning and maturing in it or it WON'T be real. Pastor and author Francis Chan says our faith needs to be like taking your first baby home: Our goal is to keep it alive. You have to know that it's real. You have to feed it, spend time with it, and nurture it. Just going through the motions doesn't work. YOU have to give time to your faith every single day. It needs to grow from a baby blanket to a parachute. When it's one you packed yourself with Jesus, you'll know you can trust it – no matter how big the leap with God. Keeping your faith alive will truly carry you through anything and everything. It won't be pretend – it will be the life saver you need.

Sit with Jesus and look up the scriptures. Note what stands out to you and write what you hear Him telling you.
Remember to note things about Jesus' character (who He is) and what He wants you to understand and do.

1 Chronicles 16:11 • Isaiah 40:31 • 1 Corinthians 16:13 • Philippians 2:12 • James 2:14

Talk to God.
Pray about what Jesus is revealing to you today about what you are pretending and how to get real.

Day 23

FOCUS

Set a new default

"For I can do everything through Christ, who gives me strength." *Philippians 4:13 (NLT)*

After leaving work one day, I tried to use my phone, but for some reason my passcode wasn't accepted. I tried again, being careful to enter the correct numbers. Denied. Not only that, I got a warning that I could only make one more attempt or the phone would be restored to factory settings and all data would be wiped out! As I was trying to process what could be wrong a co-worker called. I discovered that I had grabbed my boss's phone (which was exactly the same as mine) when I left our meeting. Man, was I glad I hadn't tried again and wiped out all his data! Sometimes, however, resetting our systems to factory settings would be best. Not necessarily our phones, but our minds.

For most of us, we have been taught the old adage, *"If you want it done right, you gotta do it yourself."* We think if we just get more motivated or muster up enough will power we can do anything. Sorry, that doesn't work. For some of us that info doesn't come as a shock — we've learned it the hard way. We tried, tried again, and then gave it one more shot (or 20 more) for good measure and it STILL didn't work out. Why not? OHHHH, because we aren't GOD. Philippians 4:13 says, *"I can do all things through Christ..."* Not on my own, but THROUGH Christ.

But how do we let Jesus fix things in us when it's obvious we have to STOP doing some things, thinking some things, dwelling on some things, and we have to START doing, thinking, and focusing on other things? How do we stop trying to fix ourselves by ourselves and let God do it...and yet still participate in the changes? You take it ALL to God — everything, every day. You have to reset your default to Jesus.

It comes down to grabbing onto every negative, wrong, bad, discouraging thought and giving it to Jesus. You simply say, *"Jesus save me! I cannot save myself from this [thought, sin, addiction, etc.] but You can and You will."* Focus on Jesus and what HE can do. Keep asking for His help even if you have to ask 50 times in a day. Reset your negatives to a positives — Jesus. Let Jesus be your default and watch Him overcome the world for you.

Sit with Jesus and look up the scriptures. Note what stands out to you and write what you hear Him telling you.
Remember to note things about Jesus' character (who He is) and what He wants you to understand and do.

Psalm 55:22 • Proverbs 3:5-6 • John 16:33 • 2 Corinthians 10:5 • James 4:7

Talk to God.
Pray about what Jesus needs to deliver you from today.

Day 24

FOCUS

Be wise without pride

"When pride comes, then comes disgrace, but with humility comes wisdom." Proverbs 11:2

Pride is one of the most common battles we will fight. We may think it's the well-educated, rich, or successful who would struggle the most with pride, but it may be even deeper in those who have not experienced many of life's accolades. For example, when the one who never went to college gets a promotion or the singer in Podunk, Nowhere gets to lead the church choir, finally having something to brag about lets us feel valuable — so we hold on tightly. We feel pride when we experience a deep pleasure or satisfaction from something we've achieved, become, or possess. Something that others admire. It happens when we feel we are over and above at least one other person in some area.

We don't typically think about it that way do we — over and above others? We like to think pride is a positive thing. Of course we should feel good when we do our best or reach a goal. Pride becomes a bad thing when it's all about us. When we dwell on how others were *"less than"* and we were *"more than."* It's a bad thing when we think, *"Look at what I have done!"* Pride takes God out of the equation.

In the Old Testament, King Nebuchadnezzar let pride be his undoing. He thought his beautiful kingdom was a result of him and him alone. He gave no credit to God for putting him in power. He could have just as easily been born into a family with nothing and no authority. God even had Daniel give the king a warning about his pride. He didn't listen and God's punishment was to make him insane for seven years. God humbled Nebuchadnezzar to show him how little man can control.

We too, are not the authors of our own lives as much as we give ourselves credit for. Only by God's hand are we allowed to have anything — including our faith, knowledge, and power. To overcome pride in your life, list some things that you are or could be prideful about. Now, as you think of each one, say these four words, *"Not I, but Christ."* Think about how it truly isn't what you do, but about what God has worked out for you. This is how you kill pride when it rears its ugly head.

Interestingly, Daniel 4 (in today's reading below) featuring King Nebuchadnezzar's story is written by the king himself. He tells how he came to understand that God is in total control, and he actually praises God for his humbling. He goes on to enjoy more than he had before, yet now with an understanding and appreciation that it's all God's doing. When our pride exits we will see wisely that God being in charge is the biggest blessing of all.

Sit with Jesus and look up the scriptures. Note what stands out to you and write what you hear Him telling you.
Remember to note things about Jesus' character (who He is) and what He wants you to understand and do.

Proverbs 16:18 • Daniel 4: 1-36 • Romans 12:16 • James 4:6

Talk to God.
Pray about how Jesus is the one to be honored in all your successes today.

Day 25

FOCUS

Remember, I love you

"For God so loved the world that he gave his one and only Son, that whoever believes in him shall not perish but have eternal life." John 3:16

For the last decade or so I have "worked" for God. When I first understood what God wanted me to do – how to use my gifts to serve the Kingdom – it was a part-time gig. I had a paying job as well. A few years ago, I knew God was telling me to leave that job and to "work" for Him full-time. Most people would refer to what I do as a *ministry* and not a *job,* but it's basically the same. I work all day, every weekday in order to accomplish what needs doing. Perhaps the big difference is that I don't work in order to make money, I work in order for God's purposes to be fulfilled.

A big part of my day is spending time with God so I know what He wants me to do. Sometimes I hear, but I don't listen. Sometimes I start out right, and then decide another way is better. Way too often I have focused on the work, the business, the finances, and the schedule more than the purpose. I hate to admit it, but I have gone for very long stretches agonizing over so many details, plans, and the future instead of the WHY. When you have worked in the "real" world the RESULT is what is important. You have to be productive and profitable or you are deemed a failure. I forget quite often that's not how God works.

Recently, I took some time off in order to prepare for Christmas. Though I knew I was pretty caught up, after a couple of days of not being at work regularly, I started to feel guilty. Somewhere in my mind I had a thought that God was probably disappointed with me. I felt like I was letting Him down or slacking off. That's when I heard God say, *"Remember, I love you. I don't just love you because you serve Me, I love you because you are my daughter. I love to see you enjoying all I have given you. I love to see you rest. I love you always."*

Sometimes we can get caught up in thinking we're only valuable if we are DOING something for God. God loves us because we're His and because we believe that His Son came to save us. God wants us to do things out of our great love for Him, not out of obligation or fear. He wants us to find joy in Him whether we are serving Him, enjoying this life He gave us, or taking a nap. He gave His Son so that we could be with Him and share in His great love story – don't forget that!

Sit with Jesus and look up the scriptures. Note what stands out to you and write what you hear Him telling you.
Remember to note things about Jesus' character (who He is) and what He wants you to understand and do.

Jeremiah 31:3 • John 6:29 • Romans 8:35-39 • Ephesians 2:4-5 • 1 John 4:18

Talk to God.
Pray about how much Jesus loves you today.

Day 26

FOCUS

Call out the lies

"When [the devil] lies, he speaks his native language, for he is a liar and the father of lies." John 8:44

I have often heard many pastors and Christian leaders who suggest taking time to be quiet so you can hear from God. Maybe I'm unique, but I often hear God best when I am doing something. Not like calculus or learning how to speak Tuyucan, but something somewhat automatic – like showering, driving, or watching a movie. I've found that when I really NEED to hear from God, sitting and stressing to listen gets me to wonder if what I hear is really Him or just me. When I'm engaged in something else and "hear" that still small voice (1 Kings 19:11-13), then I can trust it easier. God knows this about me, so he has frequently spoken to me through movie scripts.

Years ago, I was feeling very troubled and depressed. I had believed some lies about God and about myself, and while I had learned that they weren't true, for some reason, I had forgotten that. I was again living as if I wasn't changed or saved and as if God was not good or loving. God knew I needed reminding.

I turned on the TV and the movie *First Knight* with Richard Gere as Sir Lancelot was on. Julia Ormond plays Guinevere. She is the daughter of a local governor and she consoles her community after their town is destroyed by an evil ruler. He justifies his actions saying they had done something wrong (which was not true) and that they had to be punished. She stands up against his accusations and says, *"Lies! All lies!"* Then she goes on to say that she won't back down no matter what he does because she is her father's daughter.

In that moment, I heard God shouting back against the lies I was letting grab hold of me and calling them what they were – *"Lies! All lies!"* I was instantly reassured of who I am and who God is. I am no longer a victim of the past or of the lies. I am a fighter for my Father's Kingdom! That is truly who I am.

Don't you believe anything less of yourself! Call out the evil ruler and his lies that are trying to drag you down and tell them who you really are – your Father's child!

Sit with Jesus and look up the scriptures. Note what stands out to you and write what you hear Him telling you.
Remember to note things about Jesus' character (who He is) and what He wants you to understand and do.

Isaiah 30:21 • John 10:27, 14:26, 16:13 • 1 John 3:1-2

Talk to God.
Pray about what lies you've been believing and about who Jesus says you are today.

Day 27

FOCUS

Fight your fear

"I sought the Lord, and he answered me; he delivered me from all my fears." Psalm 34:4

In your brain, are two almond-shaped areas called the amygdala. The amygdala comes into play when there is something we perceive as fearful. Our "fight or flight" response activates, heart rate and blood pressure increase, and we have an unpleasant sensation of fear. This is great if the house is on fire and we need to get out, but not so nice if fear is triggered by imagined problems, worries, past memories, stress, and a host of other issues. But there is a way to fight fear.

People have studied the effects that prayer and worship have on our brains extensively. Guess what? When we spend time each day in prayer, talking to God, and worshiping Him (thanking Him, singing songs to Him, and saying what we love about Jesus) our amygdala doesn't get freaked out as easily. It's like a soothing balm to a hot spot. The more we rub that balm on, the less our fear factory produces. We simply have less and less fear.

Pastor Rick Warren says that he starts everyday by giving gratitude to God the moment his feet hit the floor. He created a list from A to Z about everything he is thankful for. Each day, he thanks God for a couple right off the bat. I did the same and a few things on my list include *Grateful to God for Kids who make our lives joy-filled and interesting, Never giving up on me,* and *Victory over fear, worry, and death.* To fight fear, a great first step is to make your own list and start each day with thankfulness and praise.

Make sure to be proactive about fighting fear and get with God everyday to talk to Him and worship Him. Throughout the day, especially if fear is creeping in, start praising God and watch fear flee.

Sit with Jesus and look up the scriptures. Note what stands out to you and write what you hear Him telling you.
Remember to note things about Jesus' character (who He is) and what He wants you to understand and do.

Psalm 56:3-4 • Proverbs 29:25 • Colossians 3:15-17 • 2 Timothy 1:7 • 1 John 4:18 • Revelation 4:11

Talk to God.
Praise Jesus today for all He's done and who He is. Then talk to Him about what that does for your fear today.

Day 28

FOCUS

Take possession

"I will instruct you and teach you in the way you should go; I will counsel you with my loving eye on you." Psalm 32:8

Remember the story of God saving the Israelites from Pharaoh (splitting the Red Sea so they could cross, miraculously providing food from heaven each day, and giving them water from a rock)? He brought them out of slavery in order to give them a new life in an area He had promised them. A place He said was, *"flowing with milk and honey."* It took them 40 YEARS to get there. The distance between Egypt and Canaan was only a few hundred miles. On foot, it should have taken less than 40 DAYS. The only reason it took them so long is because they were fighting against God instead of working *with* Him. Our success or failure will be just as critically influenced by our resistance or participation.

God has somewhere to take us. Somewhere wonderful. Yet, if we continually battle His direction, timing, process, and methods we may never get there. We can enjoy our time here or we can complain, drag our feet, worry about things, and never get anywhere close to what God promises us in the land of the living.

In order to take possession of God's promises for us, we need to do two things. **1) Cooperate with God.** That simply means we lean in, listen, and learn. We read the Bible, we ask God what we are supposed to be learning in every situation (good, bad, and hard) and we ask God how to follow Him well. We check our complaints and whining at the door. **2) Believe in His promises.** At some point we have to stop professing what we believe and actually believe God's promises. When you do that, you will find that they are true. That's when you will get to the place God is leading you — a place where you will enjoy life.

Don't waste time in the wilderness getting nowhere. Take possession of all God has for you today.

Sit with Jesus and look up the scriptures. Note what stands out to you and write what you hear Him telling you.
Remember to note things about Jesus' character (who He is) and what He wants you to understand and do.

Exodus 3:8 • Psalm 27:13 • Nehemiah 9:22-25 • Romans 8:31-37

Talk to God.
Pray about where Jesus wants to take you today.

Day 29

FOCUS

Live up to your full potential

"I am the vine; you are the branches. If you remain in me and I in you, you will bear much fruit; apart from me you can do nothing." John 15:5

I once heard someone pose a question I have never forgotten: *"What would you say if God asked you, 'Why aren't you living up to your full potential that I've created you to be?'"* Think about your answer for a moment.

In the past, I may have listed excuses and circumstances, perhaps pointed a finger at a few people. The real reason was because my life was all about me. What I wanted, my family, my friends, getting ahead, striving for happiness. The real reason was because I never went to God to find out what He had planned for my life. I couldn't live up to my full potential when I didn't know what it was, or even who I really was.

We spend a lot of time on things that we think will get us to a fulfilled life – exercising, working long hours, studying to get that degree, doting over our kids, and hanging out with friends. All of those things are important, but if we push time with God to the back burner we will never be all that God has planned for us to be. Jesus tells us that only by abiding, or being with Him, will we ever produce anything meaningful. We may contribute to life on planet Earth, but in the end it will be "burned up." Much of what we spend so much time on has no eternal value.

People go to gyms everyday, yet expend no real effort and wonder why they are still out of shape. Employees show up at work just to put in their time and accomplish nothing for their employer. People say "grace" at the dinner table every night without one thought about God. There is a level of involvement so low that there is no value in doing it. A study was done that showed that people who didn't spend at least four days a week with God (praying and reading the Bible) saw no real value. That kind of makes sense. If more days of the week are what the world puts into us vs. what we're letting God put into us, the world wins.

If you are showing up regularly with God to truly get something out of it you will. If you don't feel a connection, revelation, understanding, or closeness with Jesus then you need to check your commitment – both time and involvement. When I only went to church on Sundays, signed up to help when I thought I should, and rarely read the Bible – I missed everything. Nothing changed. Today, I love hanging out with Jesus everyday and my whole life has changed. I'm glad God won't be asking me that question. Instead, I'm longing for Him to say, "Well done!"

Sit with Jesus and look up the scriptures. Note what stands out to you and write what you hear Him telling you.
Remember to note things about Jesus' character (who He is) and what He wants you to understand and do.

Isaiah 55:10-11 • John 15:5 • Matthew 25:21 • 1 Corinthians 3:10-15 • 1 John 2:28

Talk to God.
Pray about how to live up to the potential Jesus has planned for you.

Day 30

FOCUS

Chase Life

"Jesus answered, "I am the way and the truth and the life. No one comes to the Father except through me." John 14:6

When I was about 16, some friends wanted to go swimming on the river. The plan was to boat to an area where there were inlets and the current wasn't as strong. We'd get out there to swim. My mom said no. I begged, I reasoned. She still said no. I lied and went anyway. I could have died that day.

Our river has a VERY strong current and there are treacherous undertows. People drown every year. As we got into the water the strength of the current was a little less, but I was happy to have the large tree that was sticking out of the water to hang onto. At one point I let go so I could swim around to the other side. Suddenly, the current grabbed me and I was quickly being swept away. Panic consumed me. In an effort to take control I altered my position and realized I could touch the bottom. Actually, I think God intervened. With my feet under me I was able to get back to the tree. I understood why my mom said no.

Living on planet Earth is like being on a boat in the river. Most people are just at the mercy of where the current takes them. When we find Jesus, we notice that we have oars on our boat. While it can feel difficult to paddle against the current, we see that when we keep after it we make some progress. Yet, if we stop paddling, we lose ground and find ourselves back where we started.

There is a passage in the Bible that features Jesus talking to a couple of people who said they wanted to follow Him. He basically tells the one it's not going to be easy and tells the other one something that seems kind of harsh. The man says he first needs to bury his dad. Jesus says, *"Follow me, and let the dead bury their own dead."* In Ephesians 2 it tells us that we were all dead before Jesus. He's saying that we can do a lot of things that seem good, but life without Him is where the dead are.

We have to chase life. We have to start every day following Jesus and often go against the way the world wants to take us. When we do that, we will see that not only are there oars on our life boat, there is a motor. As we focus on Jesus throughout our life's journey, we will see that He has all the power we need to get us to the life He planned for us — both now and for all eternity. To be following Jesus is to make the decision to stay close to Him and follow His leading each and every day. That's how you chase life and take hold of it.

Sit with Jesus and look up the scriptures. Note what stands out to you and write what you hear Him telling you.
Remember to note things about Jesus' character (who He is) and what He wants you to understand and do.

Matthew 8:18-22 • John 6:37-40 • Romans 15:4 • Ephesians 2: 1-10

Talk to God.
Pray about how to chase Life [aka Jesus] today and everyday.

WHAT NOW?

How to keep going on your journey with Jesus

As you may have figured out by now, if you are on planet Earth, you have places to go with Jesus. Learning how to KNOW Him and be WITH Him are just the beginning. Here are a few tips for traveling well from here on out.

Prioritize God. Be intentional in carving out time to be with Jesus EVERY day. You'll only be truly close to those you are doing life with all the time.

Keep learning. Find another study or Bible reading program to keep you engaged and learning. God's kids need to grow up. That means learning more about His Word, who He is, who you should be and how you should act.

Go to church. Find a church that has a solid foundation of teaching from the Holy Bible. You should feel at home there. Pray that God would lead you to the right place for you to worship.

Find godly friends. Following Jesus is much easier if you have people to walk with. Join a group in your church, get involved in service projects with other Christ-centered people, and pray that God would bring you a strong Christian friend or mentor that you can share everything with – including the struggles and the deep and meaningful things of life.

Fill yourself with goodness. Look for other ways to let your spirit be grown and challenged during the week. Read Christian books. Listen to Christian radio, podcasts, and sermons on your way to and from work, while you're getting ready for the day, or when you're having lunch.

Keep seeing Jesus. Don't lose sight of Jesus as you do life. Ask Him where He is in the room. See Him in your surroundings. Get used to counting on Him. Engage Him in all your decisions. Take note of what He's working on in your life. Watch Him change EVERYTHING!

TALK TO US!

We'd love to hear from you!

Once you've completed the study, we'd love to hear about your experience. Write or email us with your thoughts, questions, or feedback. May God continue to bless you like crazy as you pursue your journey with Him!

Write to us at: Being Better, P.O. Box 5105, Sioux City, IA 51102
Email us at: Contact@BeingBetter.org

NOTES & JOURNALING

Use the following pages to jot down thoughts and make notes as you'd like. Journaling is a great way to process what you're experiencing. Just write out what you're thinking and feeling – what you want to tell yourself or say to Jesus. Write your prayers, make note of what you hear Jesus telling you, tell about your progress, revelations, and hopes.

NOTES & JOURNALING

NOTES & JOURNALING